SOUL RUSH:
THE ODYSSEY
OF A
YOUNG WOMAN
OF THE '70s

SOUL RUSH:
THE ODYSSEY
OF A
YOUNG WOMAN
OF THE '70s

by SOPHIA COLLIER

WILLIAM MORROW AND COMPANY, INC.
NEW YORK   1978

Printed in the United States of America.

First Edition

1 2 3 4 5 6 7 8 9 10

Library of Congress Cataloging in Publication Data

Collier, Sophia (date)
    Soul rush.

    1. Collier, Sophia, 1956-   2. Divine Light
Mission—Biography.   3. Divine Light Mission.
4. Guru Maharaj Ji, 1957-   I. Title.
BP605.D58C64   299 [B]   77-13901
ISBN 0-688-03276-1

BOOK DESIGN   CARL WEISS

PREFACE

IF, IN 1635, THE TOWN CRIER OF KENT, ENGLAND, HAD INTONED the message now familiar in our present media—"It is ten o'clock. Do you know where your children are?"—my great-great-great-great-great-great-grandparents would have been at a loss. Their son, William Whitridge, had just crossed a great ocean and was trying to make a life on the wild and almost townless shores of America. Two generations later, William's grandchildren were probably equally confounded when their children took up the Stars and Stripes and went off to fight as soldiers against His Majesty's troops. In the eighteen hundreds, young people in my family were on the move again, rolling West in covered wagons.

I have pioneer roots. Though there are few physical frontiers left to explore, my parents have preserved this heritage for me through their independent thinking and actions on the frontier of human ideas and expression.

In the forties and fifties, my mother and father were part of the New York art scene. When I was born, in 1956, my parents were staying at the Chelsea, a famous New York hotel which is home to many writers and artists. The Chelsea was the final residence of Dylan Thomas and, had it not been for a quick ride to the hospital, the Chelsea might have been the first residence for me.

But it is not my purpose to write about my family. I want to tell the part of the story which is uniquely mine. Each of them is an individual with his or her own story to tell, or to not tell. I respect their privacy. For this reason the members of my family do not play major roles in this book except in the sense that my thoughts and adventures became possible through the confidence, free thinking, and love of life my family gave me. As a preface to my book, I acknowledge and thank my father, mother, and sister, three of my best pals.

When some people hear I have written my autobiography they look at me in surprise and ask, "What does a twenty-one-year-old have to say?" It is easy to ask this question, if you think toddlers are vacant-minded cuties and teen-agers are distinguished by their gawkiness and lack of confidence.

My book shows that it is possible to get a great deal done, even in your first twenty years. I wanted to prove through the example of my life and the lives of my close friends that the frequently baffling activities of young people in recent years have often been motivated by serious thinking and insight.

Through good fortune I am able to clearly remember most of my life right back to age three, and some incidents even earlier. I can trace my psychological and spiritual development back to my early thoughts and experiences. Since the age of eleven I have been intensely involved with the forces that have moved and shaped these times.

I have written *Soul Rush* to set the record straight, not just on why young people join spiritual and political groups, but also to give an inside view of the development of one young person's thinking from 1964 to the present.

CHAPTER

1

In many ways Georgica Beach is a beach at the end of the rainbow. It is precisely at the place where the tar of East Hampton's Lily Pond Lane ends, giving way first to green, with beach grass and wild roses growing low to the ground in clumps; then to sand; and eventually to the ocean, stretching out as far as England. Driving in to Georgica from East Hampton Village, you pass huge houses, some of them built in the 1700s by people who had already, even then, made their fortunes in the new world. Coming down Lily Pond Lane now, I always turn toward one particular house, an old, beautiful twenty-two-bedroom mansion. Now it looks imposing to me, with its fence and acres of lawn, but when I was eight years old it was just "Amy's house." Its trimmed hedges offered places for a child to hide under, stomach-down on the cool dirt like an old dog watching everything with a calm and detached eye.

One day Amy and I met at Georgica and walked the whole way down the beach to Maidstone, a beach-tennis-golf-social-eating-lazy-days-in-the-summer club to which our parents belonged. When we got there we met our friends and sat down to talk, while the wind worked at clearing an overcast sky. We got black cherry pops all around, and the conversation ranged through talk of movies and rabbits and how many times will a tennis ball bounce if you throw it in the air as high as you can. These are the kinds of things that interest you when you are eight.

Looking past my friends, I could see the ocean from where I sat. As the sky cleared it changed colors—as slowly and definitely as a watch moves—from gray-green in the overcast morning to deep blue with the clear noon.

"Let's eat now," someone said, shifting and impatient in her seat.

"No, then we'd have to wait to swim," I said, with my eyes still on the ocean.

"Oh, it's too rough," came another vote in favor of lunch.

But in my mind's eye I was already gone, in the water, bobbing up and down on the waves with the seagulls and shimmers of sunlight.

"See ya later," I said, running off to get my canvas raft and start surfing.

The water was warm and rough. When the waves broke, a strong breeze pulled the spray off their crests and blew it high in the air. I paddled out and hoped for a wave to ride, but most of them were too big. When a large set came, they broke beyond the breakers of the smaller waves. Seeing the set, I had to paddle hard, digging my arms deep into the water to make it over the crests before the larger waves broke over me.

The wind began to grow stronger. I had never been in such a rough ocean before, and all of a sudden I felt very fragile and small, with only the canvas and the air in my mat between me and the water. I decided to take the next wave into the shore. I kicked and stroked with all my might. The wave picked me up and began to rush me along high on its now-breaking crest.

I slipped down a little on the front of the wave and the crest spilled over me, enclosing me in an oval tube of water. I disappeared into the space between the inside of the wave and the place in front of the wave where the breaking crest was falling.

Out of the corners of my eyes I saw the great curved shape

of the blue wave behind me, pushing me on toward the shore. Riding on it, I could feel its power. The sun poured in through the foot of moving water above me, making it a shining green, with clear and white spots here and there. In front of me fell the white churning foam. My breathing became deep and fast. The air was rich with a fine salt spray and the roar of the breaking wave.

Then, suddenly, in a split second, everything changed, and I had an experience which shaped the course of my entire life. I slid back deeply into the tunnel of the wave; at the same time I felt as though I had slipped into suspended animation, with each of my rapidly coming breaths lasting many minutes. The roaring sound of the falling water became curiously soft and subtle. It was full of many tones and rhythms. Patterns. The air seemed thick and full of color, as if a spark had exploded, leaving a cloud of golden mist behind. I lost the sense of me as a person apart from the vast ocean and the round world it encircled.

That evening, riding home down Lily Pond Lane, I turned around and looked up over my shoulder. Swallows were dancing circles in the early evening sky. I thought about what I had seen and felt that day in the ocean. There, for an instant inside the wave, my awareness had merged with all things, but now I had returned to just being me, a person separate from all others. In trying to understand these two opposite experiences, I remembered back to the first time I had been conscious of my own individuality.

It had been the year before, in school. I had been watching some of my friends and classmates build a complex construction out of wooden blocks. As the size of the building increased, each piece was balanced—as in a card house—with less certainty upon the next.

I was sitting across the room, watching the work and trying to draw a picture of the proceedings. I felt somewhat frustrated, because when you are seven you don't yet have full control of your body. You are still not yet sure if telling your hand to turn left and twist will bring the desired amount of movement.

The block building was finally pronounced complete when one little girl stood up on tiptoes and placed an arch block atop two columns. This arch was exactly at the eye level of another, taller classmate. From my vantage, all I could see were her two eyes blinking behind the block tower.

"What she sees of the block tower would be a great perspective for my picture," I thought, perhaps wishing to make up for my lack of drawing skill with this interesting angle.

"I'll shut my eyes, and when I open them, I'll be looking out from under that arch."

But when I opened my eyes, I was stunned. I still had my drawing in front of me. I still had the same hands. On my feet were still the same socks and shoes I had put on that morning. Though I don't think I had ever tested it until then, I had always assumed that such a flight was possible: That it was very easy, very ordinary, to shut your eyes and open them up again looking out of the eyes of another person. To find out that this was *not* the way things were was quite a surprise. I yelled across the room to my friend, certain she would understand my predicament.

"Hey, I'm stuck here."

I stretched out my arms, looking at my fingertips.

"This is as far as I go."

She lay down on her back with her feet in the air like a panda bear, and after looking at her toes for a moment, she said, "Me too. Isn't it awful?"

Looking at it now, my experience on the inside of the wave seems like a "mystical" experience. But, at the time, it did not make me think about God or feel religious.

Religion, in my young mind, was one of the many baffling customs in which grown-ups tried to engage children. An already stubborn advocate of my own opinions, I made this feeling known in my kindergarten class.

Miss Grimes, the teacher, would have the children bow their heads before juice and cookies and repeat the prayer, "God is great, God is good, and we thank Him for our food." (This was private school and this sort of stuff, while illegal at public school, was considered fine there.) Then, with the praying done, it was bottoms up with the juice, and crunch-crunch-crunch went all the cookies. Every day a different student was asked to lead this dedication.

When my turn came around, I had a surprise for Miss Grimes. In my high, sweet kindergarten voice, I said, "Good food, Good meat, Good God, Let's eat."

It was certainly ecumenical. Wherever I had picked up that little prayer I don't know, but it met with an enthusiastic reception of laughter and crunch-crunch-crunch from my classmates.

Miss Grimes, on the other hand, was less thrilled. "Let's never let this happen again," she said loudly.

A few days after this incident I was over at the house of a friend, Susan Steinway, and the subject of the cookie prayer came up. Susan was sitting on the bench of the Steinway, her soft brown hair covering all but the "S" in her family name.

"You shouldn't have done that," she said seriously.

"Oh, why not?" I said, never in the mood for "shouldn'ts," especially where they concerned me and came from a contemporary. "Wasn't it fun?"

A little smile came over her face as she considered for a moment.

"I did enjoy the look on Miss Grimes' face."

But she quickly put *that* idea aside. Fun was not adequate justification for such ruckus-raising.

"But still . . ." she began.

I cut her off to get to the heart of the matter.

"Susan, I don't think that God exists."

She jumped off the piano bench and came down to sit on the floor with me.

"But who holds up the earth and keeps it going 'round the sun?" she said.

"Oh, you know, gravity. Works like magnets."

Susan leaned forward and started playing with the yarn in the rug.

"But how did it get going?"

"You mean in the beginning?"

"Yeah."

"In one big," and then I yelled so loud it brought the cook in to see what was going on, "BANG."

"But why, I mean . . ." she trailed off.

"I don't know," I said.

"See?" Susan said triumphantly. "God did it." She looked satisfied.

"Oh, come on. Just because something is a mystery, it doesn't mean God's behind it."

After a pause, I asked, "Where is Heaven, Susan?"

"Oh, it's all wrapped around after the stars end," she said, changing her mood and taking on the authoritative air of a teacher.

"But what's after that?"

"Oh, there's nothing after that!"

The next school year Miss Grimes, who had been the cause of my first theological argument, resigned from classroom teaching, having secured a job tutoring the Catholic and tamer children of John Kennedy.

At eight, you don't know much about the world, and I was eager to learn through listening and reading. I was an inconspicuous little figure in the East Hampton Public Library, sitting cross-legged on the floor, way back in the stacks, reading *Scientific American,* sounding out the hard words and looking them up in the dictionary. I was zealously following George Bernard Shaw's advice: "What should a little girl read? Anything she can get her hands on."

One thing I liked particularly about science magazines was that the authors of the various articles, as often as not, made up the biggest and hardest words. Because they had just discovered the phenomena about which they were writing, they were allowed to give them names, like happy mothers or fathers.

Since I was finding out about those big words at the same time as all the other readers, it put me on equal footing with all of them. In this way, Nobel Prize winners and eight-year-olds were equal as they both learned of *Tribingusillas noxa,* a docile germ with cousins in the flu family.

Another subject I particularly enjoyed reading about was child development. I guess it was part of the same mentality that makes actors enjoy reading their own theater reviews, both good and bad. Many of the things which I was told with confidence that "all children do" had never occurred to me. One of these things was masturbation. I learned from one author that all children did it and that it helped develop their sexuality and "yes, parents, it is nothing to be alarmed about." Then, after reading another article which claimed that masturbation was simply the worst thing for a child to do, I thought I should try it out for myself. Since, when I had tried masturbating, I had enjoyed it, I wondered at that time—just whimsically—whether it might also be true what an arrogant French novelist said: That people would never fall in love if they did not read about it in novels first.

From these books I learned that my feeling of being "stuck" when I was unable to look out of my friend's eyes was called "realization of the differentiated ego." Quite normal and necessary on the road to becoming an adult, the books said. (The "experts" seemed to agree more on this point than about the relative worth of masturbation.)

Nowhere in any of the books or in anyone's conversation did I find anything written or said about merging with the universe while you are out surfing. I had plenty of models for the "differentiated ego." People's talk was full of "you" and "me," "here" and "there," "this" and "that"—all as separate and distinct as Paris and Hong Kong. Even when people used words which attempted to capture and describe undifferentiated states, they seemed to miss the mark. "All," "everything," "the universe," seemed somehow finite. If you had "all" of something, that meant you had gathered up every last one of them and now you had them wrapped up neatly in a package called "all." "The universe" was a package into which "everything" fitted. But beyond that?

"There's nothing beyond that!" Susan Steinway said.

"Beyond that" was where I wanted to go. But on this journey with no guides or signposts, manuals or lexicons, I was on my own . . . "like a rolling stone," I sometimes thought, remembering Bob Dylan's song, which was just then becoming popular.

The next fall, when I went into second grade, my family moved our winter home from New York City to Manhasset, a nice town on the north shore of Long Island. On the school bus in the morning I often let my mind roam, pondering. The world was full of opposite edges. Edges made for separation. But what was an edge? I wondered as I watched the trees outside the school bus window.

Since it was autumn, the trees had turned bright yellow and red, green-gold and pastel brown, before they shed their leaves. In the early morning, with the sun and wind coming through them, the trees were fascinating pools of colored movement. Watching them day after day, I became fascinated with their swaying forms. It struck me that, unlike most edges, the trees' weren't rigid. I started to study them, concentrating on the line at the edge of the tree and the space directly after the tree ended. With some practice I learned to see the space *between things* as the primary object in my field of vision.

Almost everyone has had some experience of seeing things

on both sides of the line. There is a famous psychological test in which two profiles of people in white form the two edges of a black vase. Depending, literally, on how you look at things, you see either the profiles or the vase.

With still further practice, I trained my eyes and mind to see *everything*—in all three dimensions—on the other side of the line from where I normally perceived it. I spent one entire week in this reversed perception. During this time, I had no trouble negotiating my way around. If a car was moving toward me, I understood its movement in relation to me. I saw the car giving way to the space, which pushed backward in relationship to it. The most mind-boggling part of this week came when I thought about myself. According to my visual perception, my skin was not the outside covering of the distinct thing, "me," but rather, it was the inside lining of something larger. But if "I" didn't exist, who was doing all that thinking in that empty space which was formerly "me"?

Since I remained in complete control of myself during this week, and I did not tell anyone about this "hobby," it did not interfere with my schoolwork or other activities.

Then the next year, when I was ten years old, I discovered another sort of edge which disturbed me deeply because it was not something that I could change by looking at it in a different way. I was visiting my grandmother in Baltimore, Maryland. She lived in the wealthy section of town. She had a beautiful, old-fashioned drawing room, full of antiques, with the walls lined with leather-bound books and a four-by-six-foot portrait of my great-grandmother on one wall. This room opened into a small but well-cared-for garden with many kinds of roses and statues, several fountains, and at the end, a small, slate-roofed stone house which had been a play house for my mother when she was a child.

Black servants were employed to maintain this life-style. All told, my grandmother had a cook, a maid, a gardener, and a laundress. When my family was down from New York, another maid came in to serve in the dining room and, each day, to restore the house to its quiet order after the rambunctious playing of my sister and me.

At dinnertime, we all gathered around a candlelit table in the dining room. When my grandmother felt it was time to eat, she summoned the servants with a small crystal bell which she had purchased in Florence, a city she loved. Once the bell sounded, one of the maids appeared quietly from behind a swinging door with the soup course. When we were done with the soup, the little bell was rung again and the dirty dishes disappeared almost unnoticeably in the hands of the maids. They then brought out the other courses in silver serving dishes, walking around the table to offer them to each of us.

A happy and inquisitive child, I often ventured—against my grandmother's advice—behind the swinging door, through the pantry and into the kitchen. No one takes much note of a young child, so I often heard things that an older white person associated with the lady of the house would never have heard. For example, it was in my grandmother's kitchen that I first heard the joke about the old woman who was cruel to her butler. "How can you stand it?" the butler was asked. "Oh, easy," he replied. "I just spit in her soup." That joke was a real after-dinner favorite and got a knowing laugh from the colored servants of a particularly bitchy old woman up the street.

These remarks made me think that "the upper class" was kind of a sham. Although my grannie often spoke French in her drawing room so that "le domestique" would not know what she was saying, in fact "les domestiques" probably knew her more intimately than anyone.

One day, when one of the maids had to go home to get something she had forgotten, I asked her if I could come along, and she reluctantly agreed. We got on the bus and rode toward the downtown. The green trees and shaded lawns gradually passed by and gave way to row houses, and playgrounds that were nothing more than asphalt with a hoop on a pole for basketball games.

Once we were in the woman's neighborhood, we got out and walked. On the street there were old black men in baggy cotton pants and worn, sleeveless undershirts, hanging out in front of storefronts with waterstained "For Rent" signs in their dusty windows. Here and there a young mother sat on a stoop or on a wooden chair outside a row house. Around the sidewalks children played, but they moved slowly in the heat of the Baltimore June.

Finally we reached the woman's house and went inside. In the corner of the room sat an old, thin man with one leg gone at the knee. It was her father. He was eating some kind of strange food out of a tin can with his hands. When he looked up to see who had come in the door, he had no expression at all—just an empty look in his eyes which, when I saw it, made me cry.

That night I lay awake between linen sheets in a huge bed at my grandmother's house, and I wondered how that old man was resting.

CHAPTER

2

"I'M NEVER GOING TO EAT MEAT AGAIN."

I pushed aside the plate of spaghetti and meatballs I had just been served at my school cafeteria. I stood up and took off my belt.

"And I'm not going to wear leather anymore, either."

It was January, 1968. I was eleven years old, in the seventh grade at a Quaker school on Long Island. All of a sudden, something had clicked. The taste I had been enjoying in the meat was only possible because somewhere an animal had been killed and its body ground up into bits. By eating meat I was, in effect, relishing the suffering of the poor creature's death. Once I realized this connection, the taste of meat was no longer attractive to me. I knew I could live without it. After all, Gandhi and many Hindus had survived for hundreds, perhaps thousands of generations as vegetarians.

Throughout my life, I had felt strongly about the lives and spirits of animals. Once when I was about six and was walking in the woods, a wild deer with full antlers came up and stared at me nose-to-nose for several minutes. Then, with whatever curiosity had summoned him to me satisfied, he turned and walked away.

When I was about eight, my parents gave my sister a puppy. I often played with it like puppies play together, frolicking, rolling on the ground and getting into all kinds of trouble. Then, after a few years, the dog grew up and had a litter of her own. Now she related to me in a different way. She seemed to sense that I was still a young puppy, while she had grown up and was, in fact, a young mother. When I was upset on account of stubbing my toe or fighting with friends, she would come over and offer me the same comforting gestures she offered her own yowling young.

There were not many vegetarians in my circle of friends. Actually I was the only one I knew. Everybody had a different reaction to my new diet. My parents were surprised but respectful. My mother, a clever and wonderful cook, invented many meatless dishes which must have been quite nutritious, because I grew six inches that year. My father was quiet, firmly believing "she'll get over it," as he now tells me ten years later, when I am still a strict vegetarian.

When I told my decision to my friends, several of them thought they would like to become vegetarians too, if only their parents would let them. The parents, on the other hand, were most often just baffled. I remember one particular conversation I had with a friend's mother at a birthday party. I told her how I believed that animals had individual lives and characters which were just as valuable as human beings'. Agreeing wholeheartedly, she began to give me an account of her beloved Fido's moods and habits. She told me that she belonged to a humane society that protested lab experiments on animals. But she didn't see any reason why she should stop eating meat. "After all, I didn't kill it myself," she said.

I realized that the deaths of the animals she ate were very abstract to my friend's mother, although she was devoted to her house pet. The English language itself contributed to this contradiction. A cow, once killed and chopped in two, is no longer a cow but beef, a calf becomes veal, a woolly sheep becomes mutton—objects with no more sign of soul than Sara Lee cupcakes.

After the birthday party I continued to think about this conversation. What remained in my mind was the inconsistency with which my friend's mother applied her compassion. By belonging to the humane organization, she believed she was a good friend to animals. Yet her eating habits showed she was not.

Hers was not an uncommon attitude. Other grown-ups made similar remarks when I explained my reasons for becoming a vegetarian. Fine liberals, they professed a concern for life, but they still ate steak. I was shocked by how willing they were to increase their comfort at the expense of others, provided they did not have to see directly the discomfort they were causing. It seemed these people were able to justify their actions by making them abstract. I believed that if they were to concretely examine these actions they would find many of them contrary to their basic morality.

A few days later, when I was reading *The New York Times*, I realized how dangerous this capacity for self-deception was. The article which caught my attention was about an Air Force pilot who had flown a bomber in Vietnam. He said he had been proud of his technical skill in operating his jet. From 10,000 feet his bombing targets appeared to be only patterns on the earth. When he returned to his base and found that he had scored direct hits, he felt happy. He was a technician, someone who was good at his job. Only now, after returning to the United States, did he really make the connection between those patterns on the earth and what they represent in terms of human life. In his two-year tour of duty, he had killed hundreds of people and left thousands more homeless. He was now planning to join the Vietnam Veterans Against the War.

As I read *The New York Times* more regularly, I gathered the impression that confused, compromised, and inconsistent morality was business-as-usual in the adult world. Occasionally someone would have an insight into his actions and try to make amends, as this pilot did, but when property or politics was at stake, personal morality most often was put aside.

Every day I learned more about the devastating conditions in newly formed Biafra, and I wanted to do something to help the starvation victims. The war which had left them without food was motivated, as I saw it, by one thing. The area the Ibo tribe claimed as their homeland contained the richest oil fields in the region. The Ibos' insistence on their rights to this land threatened the economic interests not only of Nigeria itself, but also of other countries like England and Egypt who had stakes in the petroleum. In order to keep the Ibos and their land's oil wealth, the Nigerian government waged a savage war, financed largely by foreign oil interests. When push came to shove, the oil meant so much to the Nigerians, English, and Egyptians that they were willing to starve almost twenty million people to get it.

Although by now my political awareness has grown slightly more sophisticated and I understand that African tribal relations are often very complex, at the time, reading about the Biafran war, I felt it was simply a matter of plain greed. I wanted to help out.

I called a class meeting at school and proposed that we all fast at lunchtime and send the money we saved by not eating to Biafra. I suggested that we fast every lunch till conditions improved; others thought this was too extreme. Finally, we all agreed to fast one day. As a consolation for my compromise, I was appointed to take the money to the Biafran Relief Agency. (Already, you see, I was being offered a trade of morals for power.) The only restriction on the plan was that all the participants had to get notes from their parents allowing them to fast.

I did not respond this way to the situation in Biafra because I felt guilty about enjoying so many privileges while others suffered terrible deprivations. I knew that when you are twelve, no matter how much of a freethinker you are, there are not many aspects of your life which you control. If you refuse to open Grannie's presents at Christmas, you don't get applauded for your efforts against the American way of conspicuous consumption—you get sent to the shrink.

The school authorities were supportive of the fast, but they were less enthusiastic about my vegetarianism. This was not because they disapproved of my moral stance. It was a Quaker school and Quakers like to feel they support calls of conscience. Their disapproval came when I renounced my leather loafers for a pair of canvas sneakers, thus breaking the dress code which, though in more academic language, said, "No sneakers at school."

I love sneakers, and the first day I wore them to Friends Academy I had a marvelous confrontation with the principal, Mr. Wood. I was walking down the hall, bouncing a little as you do in sneakers. There are two reasons for this extra bounce. The first is the purely material reason that the extra foam padding in the bottom makes your walking springy. The second reason is more spiritual. In sneakers you feel free. Free not only of heavy clunks of lace-up shoes, but also free to jump higher, to run faster and, above all, to sneak around silently without the telltale clicks of your approaching footsteps giving you away.

I felt so good in my sneaks that I must have been smiling ear to ear, because when Mr. Wood saw me he looked particularly dour.

"Sophia!" he announced authoritatively, squaring himself off like a gunfighter at a showdown.

"Yes, sir!" I bounced over to him, still smiling, and noticing that he looked like a villain from a Dickens novel.

"Come to my office." He marched ahead of me. I would have marched too, but you can't march in sneakers.

He signaled me to sit down and closed the door decisively.

"Yes, sir?" I said, like the sweet little girl I was, on occasion.

"Those," he pointed fiercely at my feet, "are not allowed here."

It was perhaps at this moment that I became a yippie. Watching Mr. Wood work himself into a rage struck me as comical—all the authority of secondary education directed against a pair of sneakers. This type of ridiculous behavior was the institution's weakness. Maybe it also could become its downfall.

"But sir, you know I have become a vegetarian, and it would be hypocritical to wear leather and yet not eat meat. Do you see what I mean?"

His eyes were riveted on the offending shoes. The veins on his neck protruded.

"So you see, sir, until I get some synthetic shoes, I'm going to *have to* wear these sneakers."

He fumed.

Then I added the final touch.

"Isn't it the Quaker way to follow your conscience?"

For my thirteenth birthday, my father gave me a marvelous yo-yo that lit up when it spun.

"If sneakers bothered Mr. Wood so much," I thought in the springtime of 1968, "I wonder what yo-yos would do?"

To find out, I brought the yo-yo to school where, during breaks between classes, I enchanted my classmates with tricks like " 'round the world," "walk the dog," and "baby in the cradle."

Fancy stuff! Soon yo-yos proliferated everywhere. People were yo-yoing out the windows of the classrooms, yo-yoing in lunch lines, even in the glee club. Mr. Wood took no time in forbidding them on campus.

Why was I doing all of this? On the surface, it was revolution for the hell of it! It was making a new world with theater and enthusiasm. Inspire the troops with fun.

Yet beneath it was a serious conviction that the world needed changing at the roots. The world wasn't fun; it wasn't joyful; it in no way reflected that beautiful vision of the potential of human beings that I had had on the inside of that East Hampton wave.

It was hard to pin down exactly what wasn't quite right

about the world. The year before, at summer camp, when I was twelve, a counselor with socialist tendencies had given me Herbert Marcuse's book, *One Dimensional Man*. I studied it and was fascinated by this new world view. I went on through the fall and winter, immersing myself in Marx's *Das Kapital* and Machiavelli's *The Prince* and *The Discourses,* wherein he suggests that politics is amoral and that any means, however unscrupulous, can be justifiably employed to gain political power. I read cover to cover a thick paperback called *Patterns of Anarchy.* More than the content, I liked the title.

But books didn't satisfy me. I wanted to do something more than read and formulate my own opinions. There was something wrong with the world. I wanted to change it. As we used to say in those days, I wanted to "kick out the jams." Marcuse thought technology and capitalism were the source of contemporary problems. But, convincing as Marcuse's arguments were, I just couldn't buy his conclusions or any conclusion which blamed any or all of the -isms or -ologies for the world's troubles. Capitalism and technology were created by *people*. People want what technology and capitalism can give them. Therefore, if there is something wrong with either of these systems, it points to some deeper problem in the human psyche.

I did not want to wait until I had a position paper, a thorough intellectual analysis of "The World's Problems," before doing anything. I was ready to act now. If the problem was psychological, we needed a psychological solution. As yippies my ruckus-raising comrades and I counted heavily on something I call "intuitive response" to guide our political actions.

Intuitive response is based on the fact that at all times the brain is taking in and processing two hundred bits of information per second. This is a vast amount, much more than you could ever be conscious of, but most of this information, perhaps all of it, is stored someplace in your brain. There was, for example, a famous experiment with hypnosis in which a bricklayer's work was examined by a psychologist who discovered a slightly off-color brick which the layer had put down in a wall over ten years before. The bricklayer was then hypnotized and asked whether he could recall the brick. With alacrity and clarity he not only remembered the individual brick and accurately described it; he also corrected the psychologist's impression as to its slightly odd shape.

Although this seems like a trivial example, I believe that subtle impressions are often the most important to our understanding of a situation. "Intuition" is largely the product of associations created in the brain between subtle impressions which slipped into the mind without conscious awareness. To make use of intuition you have to trust yourself and give yourself the chance to respond to something in a way that *feels* right, even if there is no logical bridge from problem to answer which you can point to in order to justify your actions to others. Yippie acts are intuitive responses to the subtle messages of society.

Yo-yos seemed like the perfect way to undermine Mr. Wood. What could be more harmless than a yo-yo, or what could be more delightful than young people enjoying themselves in such a wholesome way? Yet to Mr. Wood it was something to be suppressed. The rigid ambience that made school a less-than-beautiful experience was drawn out, exposed, and made to look ridiculous and comical. Flowers in the barrels of guns at the Pentagon in 1967; throwing money on the stock exchange floor in 1968; Yoko Ono's nude happenings at the Statue of Liberty in 1964. All intuitive responses, psychological counterpoints to the not-quite-rightness of society.

When I explained my ideas to Abbie Hoffman, the most well-known yippie, whom I met in Port Washington in the spring of 1968, he gave me a big hug. "It's called guerrilla theater," he said. Later he wrote about meeting me and my yippie friends in his book, *Revolution for the Hell of It*: "I went to school that day on their amazing spirit. They understand this life, this America, and they are going to make this revolution."

At the end of the year at Friends Academy, I was "asked not to return." I was not very surprised, because even though I was thirteen I understood I was in the big time when I messed with Mr. Wood. But my fellow students were outraged. I had just been elected class president, unanimously. We discussed whether to burn the school down on account of my dismissal, and then we decided not to. After some reflection, I decided that this was kind of a promotion for me, because the next year I would be going to the local public school and, given my seven years of fine private school education, I would probably be able to skip a grade and thus get out of school a whole year before everyone in my Friends Academy seventh-grade class.

I spent the summer of 1969 at a camp belonging to a friend's family in the Adirondack Mountains of upstate New York. I love the geography and wildness of that region. The mountain ranges are very old, formed by glaciers eons ago. Unlike the Rockies, which are newer, the Adirondacks are smooth, with rounded peaks covered with rich brown dirt and tall trees. The earth there has a very maternal quality for me. Walking in the woods in the warm summer air, looking at the soothing green and brown colors all around me, listening to the sound of a creek and noticing moss growing on a rock where water washed over it, I felt the earth—almost as if it had a spirit—radiate pure love and peace.

I had many friends at this camp, and my summer was beautiful. I even had a summer love, which seemed a suitable way to celebrate being thirteen. His name was David and he was a tall, blond-headed boy with blue eyes. He was a talented and precocious musician who improvised intricate jazz on piano and guitar. Sometimes in the afternoons, we'd wander off in the woods, find a nice, soft place to repose, and he'd sing songs until the sun went down.

All idyllic vacations come to an end though, and come September and autumn, the trees began to turn and I went back to Long Island and revolution-as-usual. At the public junior high school in Manhasset I was a true phenomenon. While the other girls were anxiously coordinating their cardigan sweaters with their knee socks and their skirts topped with blouses and circle pins, I was just getting into wearing clothes from costume closets: period pieces from other eras, a Batman costume with cape but no cowl, and always sneakers. Nobody knew what to make of me, but after some adjustments on both sides, I made several fine friends.

One friend was named "Alpert," a black recruit from the "Valley School," the separate but unequal counterpart to Manhasset High which had been closed the year before because it hadn't conformed to court-ordered integration regulations.

The teachers thought Alpert was a terrible discipline problem. And he was. "Mentally disturbed," they said, looking forward to the day when he turned sixteen and by law their duty was over and they could expel him. Alpert threw books at teachers, yelled unintelligible oaths down the hall, and jumped out the window of the classroom to escape school after roll had been taken. I loved him and thought he was swell. Once off the school grounds, he became transformed into a gentle, good-humored person who loved to laugh and often helped out people in his community.

Another friend was "Betsy," an officer of the senior high school student body. She was in every estimation the ideal young lady, an upper-middle-class version of New York's Miss Subways. She was smart, a straight-A student, polite, well-mannered at all times, pretty, from a good family, a fashionable dresser without showing too much thigh.

I often went over to her house after school and we enjoyed each other's company thoroughly. Sometimes I thought she was very much like me, except at an early age she'd read the Machiavelli but missed the Marcuse altogether.

"James" was my best friend. He was probably the largest marihuana dealer on Long Island. Sometimes we did a little business together for mutual profit. I used to surprise the tellers at my bank by arriving at nine to withdraw three hundred dollars, then returning at eleven to deposit six hundred. That was me and James at work together.

With these friends from diverse groups at school as allies, it was hardly any time at all before I was able to stage new and bigger yippie acts. In a yippie planning meeting, there was no need to discuss ideology. If a prank idea made everyone laugh, then we knew it was the right one to do. We knew it had the proper intuitive chemistry for the situation.

Once our idea was to paint a meticulously executed rainbow on the stately arch that formed the entry way into the school. We thought it would be marvelous if, when the students and teachers came in the big oak doors under the arch in the morning, the rainbow wasn't there, then when they came back after lunch, Pooof! There it was—and such a surprise!

I want to emphasize here that we did neat work only. Though our medium was spray paint, our finished products bore no resemblance to the romantic, Greek, and sexual etchings spray-painted on cliffs around cities or in public subways.

At eleven-thirty, Betsy, Alpert, and I convened our cabal. In the huddle we decided Al and I would do the actual spraying, while Betsy would stand guard. Just as we were putting the last bit of blue in the rainbow sequence, Betsy signaled that there was someone coming—Mr. Stone, the principal of the senior high. It couldn't have gone better if I had choreographed it myself.

Al and I dropped the cans in nearby bushes and opened

the doors in such a way as to hide the lower part of the arch. Betsy engaged Mr. Stone in conversation on some highly controversial student issue which, I believe, she was just making up. As she spoke, she slowly maneuvered him through her body language back inside the school building.

"Let's go downtown," I said to Al loudly, allowing the doors to fall shut, with Mr. Stone safely inside the building.

"All right!" he said, and we left the scene of the crime.

"Do you smell paint?" Mr. Stone asked Betsy. She sniffed and made a face.

"You know what that is?" she said. "Mimeograph fluid. The machine in the student office doesn't work, you know."

We finished the rainbow at night, but later it was sandblasted off. I guess the town authorities did not agree with our views on public architecture. But we didn't just do our yippie work in the school; by 1969 we had expanded our operation to the local government as well.

One day James and I were walking home from school when we started talking about the Chicago Seven trial. We had always heard that young people should take more interest in government, and so we had an idea for a little something we could do to improve our own town of Manhasset, Long Island. We both agreed that street confrontation was not a very good tactic. We, unlike the rest of the country, knew the FBI was very active in the underground political left. We even kidded our friends when they got carried away with radical rhetoric: "Hey, what's the matter, you joined the FBI?"

"Well, what about a coup d'état?" James said. "Coups work like this: You just replace the top of the government with your own people, and you count on the bureaucracy to go on plodding along in their machinelike predictable way. Clerks aren't really that choosy about whose papers they file. You know?"

"So I see," I said, possibly a little stoned. "The idea is to detach the leadership from the bureaucracy and put in new leadership . . . hmmmm." My mind went to work on this idea.

"No, I don't think that will work here. I think a coup would insult Americans, no matter how much better was the leadership that it brought in. Coups work in countries where people don't think much about government; where there are fewer people who know how to read. Look, Americans pull off their own coup every four years at election time. Elections effectively detach the politicians from the permanent bureaucracy. So, for this reason, it is not presidents who have the power, it is the clerks, the little office messengers, the secretaries. They are the ones who are in the government over a long period of time. So, I think the thing to do is to radicalize them and then *they* can manipulate the short-time leaders."

Just at this point in our conversation we came to the town office. "Let's go in and see what 'they' think about this," James said. It was four-thirty in the afternoon, and the only people around were just the people we wanted to see: two young clerks. On their desks were the symbols of power: racks of rubber stamps with signatures of town officers, stamps that said, "O.K.," "Passed," "Rejected," "Check Clear to Cash." Clearly we were talking to a couple of very powerful people in the town of Manhasset.

We spent that day just making friends, and we went back every few days and explained to the two clerks their true position in government. After a month or so, our little band expanded to six when two black janitors joined our discussions.

"Yes, ma'am, we know everything that goes on here. We read them memos in the trash."

A bookkeeper joined our group. "Need a little money? I'll post it to you."

And our latest convert to power was a file clerk. "If I want to, I can take so long to get some information from the archives that the officer's term will have expired before he can do a thing. On the other hand, I can also get it for you in an hour."

The culmination of our efforts came when we all got together and smoked some hashish in the judge's chambers—without him, of course—all of us aware that he was in an elected office, and that he was nothing without us.

On some missions, I worked alone. For my own neighborhood, I devised a program of loving vandalism. The program began as an on-the-spot inspiration. One evening, as I was walking down the street carrying a large, crosscut bow saw, I rounded a bend and noted, looming in front of me, a big sign that said, "Strathmore-Vanderbilt Country Club," with a large arrow on which was written "private." The country club itself was several miles from this sign. How pretentious, I thought, to advertise your privacy. With a quick look right and left, I whipped the saw into action. Thirty seconds later the sign was lying flat on the ground.

They put the sign back up. It fell again. Back up. Back down. Police guarded it, but when they turned their heads —"Timber"—the sign was down. After that it was not put back.

Another evening I was bicycling home, carrying several gallons of white paint. (It's always good to be prepared.) Outside one of the houses I passed there was a little cement figure in the shape of a slave, with black skin and dressed in white rags. With a brush, I dabbed white paint on the face, hands, and feet. The next evening I returned with peach-colored pigment and did the rags over in saffron. Now it appeared the lantern was held by a Hare Krishna devotee.

Back at school, I had petitioned to skip the eighth grade, and at the end of October 1969 I got the O.K. Somehow, though, my classwork still did not have compelling interest for me. It wasn't that it was so bad, really. It was just that other things were better—more fascinating and meaningful.

Back when I was eight, conducting my research into the nature of the universe in the East Hampton library, I had run across a tiny article in a magazine about a substance called LSD. I was fascinated by the idea of "a chemical that changes perception." I thought, I've got to get hold of some of that. Now, four years later, LSD was changing my perceptions of school. Once while I was tripping at school I had a remarkable revelation, so much so that I was inspired to deliver to my astonished ninth-grade math class an extemporaneous speech about a relationship I had just seen between Shakespeare and the binomial theorem.

In French class, when the teacher spoke, acid let me *see* the sound. The French "r" of *parler,* the verb "to speak," came rolling out through the air in light blue, looking like a painting of a wave at the foot of Mount Fuji.

Sitting on a staircase while classes changed, I watched the frenzy of color and motion stirring past me, a parade of people. Then, when they were gone, I looked at the tile floor, full of the scuffs of a thousand feet passing.

A scuff on a tile is a three-dimensional formation, with the scuff mark being a little higher than the tile. For several minutes, this relationship became particularly marked, until it seemed that the scuffs were raised several inches off a completely clean tile floor and looked like wisps of smoke. This perception made me reflect on the nature of time: Somehow there was in creation a forever-clean surface on which events occurred and passed like wisps of smoke, scuffs on the tile floor.

Grown-ups wonder why young people take drugs. At Manhasset High the administration was so upset about the students' drug consumption that they hired a specialist, the ex-assistant director of Odyssey House, the heroin rehabilitation center in New York City.

James and I were assigned to be in a group with this specialist and some of the other students. We were supposed to talk about our problems with life and drugs. I couldn't relate to this approach. I could see that there were kids for whom drugs acted as a numbing agent which helped them deal with the pain of bad family lives and the oppressive school system. But for me, James, and many of our friends, taking drugs was an engrossing adventure, a means to observe life and go beyond our existing view of life.

The only kind of drugs I ever took were hallucinogens, like LSD and marihuana. One of the main things these drugs seemed to do for me was separate me into two "me's." The first me was the traditional me, the one who walked around all day doing things, and the second me, the new me, was the one who just watched. It was the sort of thing Thomas Merton might have loved: Finally a clear line between action and reflection.

I started to call the reflective me the "New Mind," because with it I scrutinized the behavior of the everyday me in a fresh way. Observing with the New Mind, I learned a great deal about the workaday habits by which I—and most people —conducted our mental business.

The normal way for the everyday mind to process information was to analyze it quickly and file it. Then, whenever I had to deal with the same or similar information, I would not have to rethink my conclusions, I would simply dip into my mental file and pull out a ready-made opinion.

This method of thinking would be fine if the original filed analysis were perfect—if it took all the facts into account and was free from any bias. But when the New Mind started looking through the everyday mind's files, it was apparent that this was not the case.

In my case, for instance, "chopsticks" might have been filed under "Impossible to use" and Brooklyn under "Who'd ever want to live there?" The limitations of these conclusions were immediately clear. If it were not for the New Mind intervening with flashes of insight and creativity, I would probably never go to Brooklyn or try to use a pair of chopsticks.

The workaday mind's problems were compounded in the social sphere. When people spoke to each other, I noticed, they really did not try to understand what the other was saying. When they heard something that sounded similar to what was in their own mental files, they thought they knew exactly what the other meant, even when they didn't.

The New Mind operates with compassion and detachment, and it is enlightening to encounter it, through whatever means. Though I felt drugs were not the best means of getting into the New Mind, they did provide me with many insights. Fresh from such an awesome frontier, is it any wonder I found the drug rehabilitation group impossible to relate to?

By the time spring came around in 1970, I felt a real change in mood. At first I thought it was just in me, that my yippie feeling was in its diminuendo days. But then I also saw a change in the people around me. Many of the junior high school students who had been baffled by me the past September were now getting into the act. Skirts and nylons were giving way to denim jeans. Guys' hair grew longer. The beer crowd was asking me where to buy dope.

When the Kent State confrontation occurred in 1970, all these novitiates wanted to protest by having a large demonstration. Even though I helped them organize a 5,000-person gathering, this sort of politics was not my intuitive response. Something new was in the air. The whole mood of the times was changing.

I applied and was accepted to an innovative boarding school in Arizona. It was the first school I personally found and chose for myself. Then, with the summer just starting and the green-gold on the trees deepening in tone, I packed up my stuff and headed off for a summer on a silver lake in the Adirondacks.

CHAPTER

3

I STOOD HIGH ABOVE THE DESERT FLOOR ON A RIDGE, LOOKING out across the canyon and listening. The wind made a hollow, soft sound as it moved among the huge rock formations. The rocks were sandstone, colored deep red like terra-cotta. Below me on one side were the dotted shapes of the many scattered buildings of my new school, Verde Valley. On the other side was the wild, dry red desert, ranging off as far as I could see. Inside the dorms, students were unpacking. Since my roommates had not yet arrived, I had gone off exploring in these nearby hills. I was fourteen years old and starting the tenth grade.

It was new to be here, in Arizona. This year, 1970, I was going to be away from New York and New England in the fall. I liked this part of the country. It was vast, quiet, and old. There was a richness in the dry air and a peace in the ancient rock.

My mind sailed off into the open space of the canyon. By the time I looked down again at my immediate surroundings, I noticed that the cool shadow had moved several inches along the warm ground. An hour, maybe two, had passed. I looked back down at the school.

Verde Valley had been operating for twenty-five years, founded by an old-fashioned gentleman named Hamilton Warren. He had bought this spectacular piece of land, signed up some students, and, with the help of some friends and

Hopi Indians, begun to build. His idea was bold and unique for 1945. Across the Atlantic, one of Ham's friends, A. S. Neill, was just getting his own school together, a school which later came to be known as Summerhill. Barry Stevens, a good friend of the Gestalt psychologist, Fritz Perls, was at Verde Valley during this formative period, and she describes it in one of her books, *Don't Push the River*.

This pioneering, build-your-own-school attitude did not end when the first school buildings were finished. Each year the students and faculty expressed the changing zeitgeist of the larger world in some new project. In the middle sixties, students and teachers made great efforts to recruit and insure scholarships for people from diverse ethnic groups. Now, in 1970, with the ecology movement in full swing, student interest turned toward trash. Verde Valley's campus was a small model of the larger world, creating organic, paper, and metallic waste at quite a volume. Figuring out the best ways to minimize these wastes and dispose of them in an ecologically sound way was a project that consumed much mental energy. Several students invented a marvelous makeshift incinerator that burned hotter, better, and with less smoke than the store-bought models. There was no shortage of willing volunteers for trash sorting. My main contribution to the ecology effort was in the area of saving water, a crucial concern to a community in the desert. I figured out that the toilets with tanks were using an unneeded gallon with each flush, so I gathered up bricks and large stones of the size which would displace about a gallon of water, and put them in the tanks. In the course of the school year this action saved about 25,000 gallons of water.

Verde Valley School was like a Phillips Exeter for free spirits. Its Phillips Exeter quality was apparent in the emphasis on high standards of classroom work. On the curriculum of the lower grades was the traditional assortment of "English Composition," "Algebra I and II," and other subjects familiar to all those who went to high school. For the higher grades, there was a more diverse menu: "Semantics," "Philosophy of Religion," "Anthropology," . . .

The free-spirit quality, however, was mainly the result of the kinds of students the school attracted. Although they were all of high-school age, ranging from fourteen to nineteen, most of the students had already formed distinct—often charming—personalities. They were people who liked to do their own thinking and share their thoughts through a variety of media.

In the senior class were the sons of the actors, Jack Lemmon and Walter Matthau, and together they made a younger version of the "Odd Couple." In my class there were three people who would inherit a million dollars or more each when they turned twenty-one, though you would never have known it from these future millionaires' style and appearance. For the most part, they seemed like regular, confused young people in Levi's. Hanging around with these folks, I began to see that many of them had used their backgrounds in a surprising and liberating manner.

It is often assumed that such a wealthy or powerful background might be a burden for a young person. People think it must be easy to get lost among all those family portraits, struggling with the legacy of your famous and beautiful parents. While this may be true in some cases, I began to get a different picture from being in the company of so many young heirs. Many people do not realize the opportunity this sort of background provides a young person. It gives them the opportunity to "graduate from the upper class."

This graduation is more spiritual than material. It allows you, if you are one of them, to begin to live more freely, unfettered (spiritually, not materially) by the struggle for power, money, and prestige that consumes the lives of so many people. I don't mean to say that because you are rich you don't have to worry about money, because you've got all you need. If, however, as a child you already went to all the finest schools, had all the finest clothes, already had flown in a Learjet, already had all the doors open to you socially, then you are in a prime spot to notice, as they say in *Godspell,* that "center-on-the-beach/cushion-on-the-seat" are not all they are chalked up to be. They are not the aim of human life. Once attained, these luxuries do not hold any ultimate fascinations. When you realize this, you've graduated, you're free to pursue anything in the whole world that interests you, without regrets, questions, or doubts. You can even give up having any money, to be like Buddha, swap clothes with a beggar, and find the ultimate joy of your life sitting under a tree.

Despite all the interesting activities and companions, and despite the fact that Verde Valley was probably the school most suited to my temperament and intelligence, I still didn't really want to be at school at all. As had happened before, I was finding myself drawn in directions other than the ones prescribed by the prevailing authorities. A literal example of this came one day on my way to French class. I started out from my dorm extra early so that I could walk to the classroom part of the campus by way of the "scenic route" on the outskirts of the school.

As I rounded a bend, there was a large, dry tumbleweed in the middle of my path, rocking slightly in the breeze as if it were a runner poised at the beginning of a race. I stopped and looked at it, remembering the teasing ways of the airborne star of the French children's film, *The Red Balloon.*

"Okay, I'll race," I said aloud. "You say go."

In a minute the wind picked up with a *Whooosh!* and the tumbleweed rolled into an easy lead. Up over the hill, down the road, and into an arroyo (a wash cut by the water of many years' spring rain) I ran ramble-tamble after the rolling tumbleweed. In the wash there were many large stones to dodge and hurdle. While I was jumping, spending half my time coming up and down, the tumbleweed sailed over the obstacles on its own road of wind. I arrived at my French class rather late—exhilarated but nonetheless a loser.

My teachers were quite sympathetic to me. One of them, the head of the English department, Ingebord Lang, was particularly determined to help me enjoy being at Verde Valley. A sagelike woman in her sixties, she reminded me in many ways of Lillian Hellman, a persistent survivor, both gentle and strong with a touch of something else—a little irony, just a bit on the joyful side of bitterness.

One day, Inge, as we called her, invited me over to her house, and after I had sat down she point-blankly said, "You hate sitting in the classroom, don't you?" After a long talk, she said she would convince the other faculty members that I should be exempt from classes for the rest of the year, making my academic progress in another format.

"I'm respected around here," she said. "There'll be no problem. Watch out for people; everybody has his own opinion of what is right and proper for you to do with your life. But nobody knows, nobody but you."

She spoke from experience. "You have to watch out," she said again. Lighting a Camel, she paused and looked off into the desert. Her face was serious.

"In the fifties I was a postmaster in a little town east of Brattleboro, in Vermont. After a time, I started to notice that my mail was coming in on top of the stack every day. Look, you can't go reading the postmaster's mail like that and not have her notice. Then the letter arrived. I was on McCarthy's list."

She looked at me and with a note of her usual good humor, she said, "That's Joe, not Gene."

I nodded.

"I was months on that case." Her wind-weathered, sun-browned hands trembled slightly as she recalled a family member who testified against her.

"She told them, 'Oh, yes, Inge's a communist, she's a Christian Communist. She's always for the underdog.' This is what went on in our Congress."

She took a long draw on the Camel and began talking about other things.

Inge was right about the effect her sponsorship would have on my proposal to stop going to class. She arranged a program for me where I intensively studied two subjects in which I was very interested: English and biology. For English, I was to come to Inge's house once a week and let her read and correct whatever I had written. For biology I had a similar arrangement. After some initial lab work I was to concentrate on molecular biology—the study of the large molecules that make up living things—mostly through independent study, while meeting with the biology teacher twice a week. Biology fascinated me, and I immediately found myself back with the pages of *Scientific American*. Research starts with wonder, Aristotle said, and in molecular biology I found many things to wonder about.

I have a friend who sends me *The New York Times*, here and there, whenever I am away from the East Coast. When he heard that I was studying biology, he sent me one of his infrequent and cryptic messages with the next copy of the newspaper. It read: "How does the golden plover know where to fly? No theories, please." After a bit of investigating, I found that this was a very good question, but unfortunately all the available answers were just theories. It was in this way that my Zen friend, fan of *The New York Times*, sent me off in a whole new direction in my life.

Golden plovers hatch in the northernmost parts of Canada and Greenland during the short arctic summer. After some months, as the temperature cools, they begin a 6,000-mile journey to the more hospitable shores of southern Argentina and Uruguay. The youngest birds, those born only that year, do not grow in their flight feathers in time to depart with the elder, experienced members of their flock, but are forced by nature to wait a full three weeks to begin. By the time the young plovers are ready to leave, all the birds that have flown the route before are long gone, and the young are left to find their way alone.

And they do. Every year the young plovers find their winter home with the older birds of their flock in the warm sun of South America. Imagine it. One day they are pecking about on the shores of some high Canadian inland lake and the next day they are off soaring over the ocean with great endurance and confidence. Indeed, the plover has no room for wondering when the cold gray waters of the Atlantic are meeting the pale blue horizon on all sides.

So how did the plover know where to fly; what could I tell my friend who sends me *The New York Times*? Jung, though he may not have known any plovers, gave me an idea about where I could find out. In a lecture of his, "The Structure and Dynamics of the Psyche," he said:

> The collective unconscious, as the ancestral heritage of possibilities of representation, is not individual but common to all men, and perhaps even to all animals, and is the true basis of the individual psyche.
>
> This whole psychic organism corresponds exactly to the body, which though individually varied, is in all essential features the specifically human body which all men have. In its development and structure, it preserves elements that connect it with the invertebrates and ultimately with the protozoa.
>
> Theoretically, it should be possible to "peel" the collective unconscious, layer by layer, until we come to the psychology of the worm or even the amoeba.

It sounded like an interesting journey, layer by layer. At least then I might have something to tell my friend who sends me *The New York Times*.

For a classroom in which to study and ponder these subjects, I had the vast desert. Every day I gathered up my books in a little rucksack and went off, climbing high up into the red rocks. I stopped and stayed where I found a cool shadow or a gentle cave in the sculpted sandstone.

While the weather was warm, I occasionally went out on "solos," excursions whose name reflects the influence of the Outward Bound program on Verde Valley. In the most strict Outward Bound solo you would go alone and stay in the wilds for several days with only a notebook. I, radical about many things, was only a liberal on solos. I took food and reading material, but no friends.

On one occasion, during this period when I was thinking about the golden plovers, I went on a solo and my research, begun with wonder, took on new dimensions. I hiked far back into the high country, where it was profoundly quiet. I wore few clothes and, to avoid sunburn, I had rubbed red dirt all over my exposed body. By midday it was very hot and I stopped in the meager shade of a juniper tree.

After some time a wasp came buzzing by. It circled my head and came down to light on my upturned palm. Strangely, I was unafraid that it would sting me. I held my hand still and stared fixedly at it.

I concentrated on its head and then its eyes. Gradually every detail on its face became very pronounced, as if I were seeing it through a microscope. It did not appear enlarged in relation to the rest of the things I could see, but rather the details were very, very clear. It seemed as if I had put on a pair of very powerful glasses that revealed the minutest lines and subtlest shadows of shading and color: My vision changed from its usual 20:10 down to the impossible resolution of 20:1 inch.

The wasp's eyes looked like Bucky Fuller's geodesic domes. I could see each individual facet on the surface. In my mind's eye I remembered the shapes of honeycombs.

After a few minutes, I changed the focus of my own eyes from the wasp in my hand to the rocks in the distance. Though this change in focus happened in an instant, as a reflex, the time it took my eyes to respond seemed long. I was very sensitive to and aware of the feeling across my lens, as it stretched to make a new, thinner shape through which to view the distance. I also felt my iris move, contracting to take in the greater light.

Once my lenses and irises were still, I saw an amazing and awesome sight. In front of me were all the familiar things: the rocks and cactus, scrub oaks and juniper trees, all hues in the shades of the familiar spectrum, but also there was a *new color*. It was something I had never seen or heard of before. It was a new color, and many things were etched in it.

I gasped, astonished. My body jolted in surprise and then there was a sharp sting on my hand. Reflexively, I slapped over to the pain. In that instant, the new color was gone; the wasp lay dead on the ground. I sat still against the gnarled trunk of the juniper for a long time, sucking on my palm where I had been stung.

The new color I had seen was one of the most beautiful experiences I have ever had, yet when I saw it, I felt an instant of doubt. In a nano-second of time, too quick for these thoughts to become conscious, my mind had rebelled. In a nano-second of protest, it had said, "Wait, this is not possible. Remember 'ROY G BIV.' There is only *R*ed-*O*range-*Y*ellow-*G*reen-*B*lue-*I*ndigo-*V*iolet."

And it was in that nano-second that I gasped, that the wasp stung me, and that my vision of this beautiful new part of the world was gone. Real as red, I'd seen a new color, but because of a moment of disbelief, it had disappeared. Disbelief, the self-fulfilling prophecy.

I had previously been aware of my own psychic potential for meanness and a certain laziness of my "action mind"; but this was the first time I realized there was a part of my mind that resisted new experience. It was like having an American Legion outpost in my own head.

In my workaday set of values, I had always thought I was very open to new experiences of perception. And now, sitting up against the juniper, with everything appearing normal ROY G BIV again, a feeling of well-being came over me as I accepted what I had seen. If this is crazy, I'm delighted, I thought. I've always loved color. Sometimes when I am slightly drunk, I look at brightly colored things and feel I can almost taste the color, it becomes so rich for me. From the extraordinary perceptual experiences of my childhood and from my experiences on LSD, I had learned to accept whatever I saw and sensed, using it, as one does fiction or theater, to give greater meaning to my day-to-day sensations.

In this case, though, I thought this was more than a hallucination. Perhaps it was a crack into the universal collective unconscious and, through some inexplicable but marvelous workings of nature I had, for a moment, actually seen as the wasp did. Of course, after I had killed him, his eyes no longer saw, so neither did mine. After the swelling from the wasp's sting went down on my hand, I made a note in my journal: "Find out if wasps can see in ultraviolet." Apparently they do.

Though I had no trouble accepting what I saw, *after* I had seen it I was still disturbed by the nano-second of disbelief I had felt. Several days later, back at school, I still could not shake this sense of disquiet, knowing there was a part of my mental processes that were working against the ends I desired most—to live in the most expansive realm of experience and understanding.

I had heard about a series of experiments concerning something called "habituation." In these experiments people were given decks of cards which had reversed colors: red spades, black hearts. The people perceived the cards to be normal, their minds lazily presuming the black hearts were spades and the red spades were hearts. Everyone knows red is hearts; black is spades. So why look again?

"Goddamnit! You could miss your whole damn life because of habituation," I told Eliot, my boyfriend, one day shortly after I had returned from my solo.

I wanted to live with eyes wide open, not to miss a thing. I wanted to become a permanent denizen of "Edge City," a name invented by Ken Kesey to describe such perennial openness. On Kesey's bus in which his "Merry Pranksters" had traveled, there was a motto, "Further, Further" emblazoned on the front bumper to remind them that their destination, Edge City, could be continually achieved.

On my own personal bus ride, "further, further" meant gaining control over the parts of my mind that were working against me, inhibiting my internal freedom. Once I started thinking about just which parts these might be, I found them everywhere. Right for starters there was the reactionary force, habituation, that kept me from seeing and accepting new experiences. Then there were other things: selfishness, greed. . . . I needed work in the most basic areas. It was simple stuff: an attachment to food, for example. Have you ever "pigged out": become so full of desire to eat that you go to the fridge and stuff yourself to a point way past good sense? You can pig out on other things besides food. Try sex. The list is endless.

After a few days of noticing all the faults I shared with the rest of humanity, I became quietly sad. Such a long journey lay in front of me and, among all my friends, I did not feel that there was one of them with whom I could talk it over. It wasn't that nobody cared, it was just that nobody knew. The discussions I had with friends, though often charged with enthusiasm for the journey "further, further," reminded me of the time in kindergarten when I had yelled "I'm stuck" across the room to a classmate, hoping for some advice on how to regain my freedom. The only answer I received was a resigned, "I know. Isn't it awful?"

With little help coming from the outside, I realized I would have to turn to my own internal resources in the effort to expand my awareness. I decided to adopt several forms of austerity to train and discipline my mind. One part of my new plan was weekly fasting. I chose Monday and Thursday as days to abstain from all foods except tea. Another part was a program of physical self-discipline. I often went running for long distances in the desert, trying to surpass my feelings of tiredness and break through into greater self-control.

Very quickly my way of living began to change. Aside from the fasting and physical regime, I was careful in my speech and tried to be neat, punctual, and hardworking. At school I signed up for the undesirable but necessary chore of potwashing. My approach was somewhat similar to that of Ben Franklin. He made a list of all evil human propensities, horrors like anger and sloth, and balanced them out with good and Christlike qualities, like temperance and cleanliness. Then he fastidiously rated his day-to-day performance on a scale of one to ten. Though we were working on similar areas, I believe my purpose was quite different from his. I did not feel that the virtues I was trying to develop were ends in themselves. If, through fasting, I actually was able to break my attachment to food, the victory would not be one of prudence over gluttony; instead, it indicated progress: I was learning to control my mind.

The same warm weather which set me off on the "solos" in the desert also stirred in me a desire to make some wider peregrinations to other more populated areas. One morning, without telling anyone but Eliot, I went off hitchhiking to a small former ghost town. Once a booming mine town, it was now the home of many families of retired hippies. Several months before, I had met a fellow whose brother lived there, and he had given me a detailed description of how to find his brother Jess's cabin.

After a day's journey, I arrived in the little town and loved it immediately.

"You want to stay here?" the young "semi" driver who gave me a long ride asked in amazement as I swung down from the cab.

"Sure," I said, smiling, thinking it was much better than

taking him up on his offer to travel with him and his load of frozen turnips to Seattle.

Looking around, I felt everything had the quiet peace of a long-abandoned junkyard: Tall grass and wildflowers at the bases of huge metal things rusting in the sun; houses of aged brick, a gentle, warm breeze passing through their glassless windows. I sat down against the fender of an old car and played a little harmonica before I made my way up to Jess's cabin.

Jess was a huge person with a big, reddish-brown full beard and lots of reddish-brown hair. He wore faded blue overalls with patches, and no shirt over his large, strong arms. His face was tanned, and in general he seemed the picture of healthy, vital energy.

I said hello, and soon tea water was on the woodstove.

"How is my little brother?" he wanted to know. "Yes, please stay. Emily, give her a quilt. Please feel at home."

The cabin was very snug and homey. After we had been talking a while, I asked, "How do you make your living?"

A look came over his face as if he had just remembered something. "Well," he said, "we are very interested in herbs."

"Oh? Is it lucrative?"

He stood up, smiled, and out of his pocket pulled a gold watch on a long, gold chain, clicked it open and said, "We get by. Listen, I've got something I should do right now. Excuse me?"

"Sure," I said, with visions of him going to wash the water on the growing alfalfa sprouts or to grind some homegrown wheat into flour. I followed Emily and him onto the porch, which faced out into a great gravel pit which had once been a mine. Sitting down in an old rocking chair, I watched the two of them slip and slide down the steep sides of the pit and disappear into a wooden shack at the bottom.

While I was sitting on the porch I thought about Emily. She was a pretty girl with blonde hair and deeply tanned skin. A week or so before I had arrived, she had just come back to civilization for the first time in two years. She had been living in the wilds of a closed-off canyon, subsisting on a diet of herbs and roots.

Shortly after Emily and Jess went into the shack, I saw some other figures making their way down the other side of the pit, also disappearing into the shack. Feeling a bit bored, I decided to go down there also. I opened the door quietly. Jess was sitting on an old chair, talking into an ancient telephone.

"Shhh," Emily said, when I started to speak, "he's talking to London."

I sat down. The other men were labeling large, overstuffed plastic bags with various people's names. Jess hung up the phone. Turning to Emily, laughing and shaking his head, he said, "They didn't want us to send them dope, they wanted us to send them Coors beer." Then he turned to me and gestured toward the bags with his thumb: "Herbs, very lucrative."

Often during the day I climbed up on a billboard that overlooked a nearby road and, in the distance, the long, flat, sandy plains. Sometimes Emily joined me, and we talked about her life in the canyon. This was a momentous time in her life. A few days after I arrived, she and Jess climbed into his '47 Ford Powerwagon pickup truck and drove several hours into the city. There they bought her a complete set of luggage, new clothes, cosmetics, and perfume. She had finally made her decision. She was going back to Cambridge to marry that old Harvard man after all.

Then, after a week, I felt it was time to go back to school. Jess was sorry I was leaving. Since I'd become a real part of the family in the short time I was there, Jess related to me as if I was his little sister. Actually, I think this was the way he related to almost everyone. In his dope-dealing business he made a fantastic amount of money, which he doled out to his indigent, spaced-out friends all over the country. Like the new age Godfather, he had decided to take responsibility for them all.

When it was time to leave he picked me up and hugged me.

"Here's a little present," he said, handing me a bag of peyote. "Good for the head," he said with the smile of a doctor.

Then we got into his old truck and he drove for a day, taking me back to school.

Once back at Verde Valley, I typed up an outline for a plan by which I could skip the eleventh grade by going to summer school that year. When I took it to the headmaster, he read it and said in a slightly acerbic tone: "At least with this we know your plans in advance."

CHAPTER
4

WE SPED NORTH TOWARD UTAH, TRAVELING THROUGH ARizona's Painted Desert with its bright-colored streaks and layers of sand and rock. I was going to the Hopi reservation to live for a month, on a school-sponsored field trip. At this time of year all the students at Verde Valley School had a chance to get out into the larger world and experience a little life beyond their textbooks. Outside the window was Navaholand. In the distance, here and there, muted by the dry haze on the horizon, we could see a *hogan,* the traditional Navaho dwelling place formed from wood beams with a roof of dried mud. Occasionally there was a Navaho walking with a small herd of sheep.

The Hopi reservation is spaced over the tops of three mesas. These are jutting mountains of rock left over from another era when water had cut through these canyons. The total area of Hopi land is like a small splinter in the larger lands of the Navaho. This is not a new arrangement, and the Hopi prefer it this way. In the time before the white people came, the Navaho and the Hopi had been traditional rivals, owing perhaps to their different modes of living: The Hopi was a farmer and the Navaho a nomad. Even today, in the Navaho's concession to agriculture, they choose husbandry, a profession in which it is still easy to roam. The Hopi, on the other hand, have always been settlers, working their plots of dry desert land into fields that grow an abundance of hardy food to support them.

Before bulldozers made roads to the flat tops of the mesas, it was easy for the Hopi to control who came and went. When the Navaho or other nomadic tribes arrived at harvest time to share by force in the food, it was easy for the Hopi to see them approaching and kick them down the mesa's steep walls to their reward on the rocks below.

During my month in Hopiland I was supposed to stay at the house of Thomas Banyaca and his family. Thomas was a middle-aged Hopi who traveled around the United States and spoke on the Hopi prophecies ("Now is the time . . ." his lectures began, year after year) and the ecological danger the white people were inflicting on the world. According to Hopi legend, Thomas said, the white brother was separated from the Hopi at the time of creation. The white brother then traveled east, away from the spiritual center of the universe, which just happened to be in Old Oraibi, on the third of the Hopi mesas, a few hundred yards from the Banyacas' kitchen. When the white settlers came, they were welcomed as family, "But then . . ." Thomas trailed off, with eyes of betrayed faith.

In spite of the spiritual danger coming from the white civilization, Thomas saw no problem in using all the technologies of the modern world. "It is our spiritual heritage which makes us Hopi," he said, while riding around in his son's souped-up Charger. Also staying with Thomas were two macrobiotic women who, through brown rice, were seeking to cure Thomas's sister of various maladies, including old age. A friendly, zany hippie-professor often dropped by and shared a healing preparation from his own cultural tradition: chicken soup.

Thomas's house was built partly in the Hopi style, with fitted stones for walls and round logs for a ceiling, and partly in a more familiar way: two by fours, sixteen inches on center, covered with sheetrock, gypsum mud, and paint.

Not too far from Thomas's house stood another, painted pink and quite out of place on the Hopi reservation.

"Who lives there?"

Nobody would tell me. I finally found out from one of the BIA (Bureau of Indian Affairs) workers, an Indian equivalent of an Uncle Tom. In the pink house resided Elizabeth White, Thomas's sister, who many years before had converted to Christianity. She was renowned by museums and anthropologists for her exacting work in making traditional Hopi coil pots from native clay. "It is our crafts which makes us Hopi," she said, winding her coil pots one after the next.

Hopi religion is an Indians-only affair, despite what Frank Waters wrote in *The Book of the Hopi* and *The Masked Gods.*

"Yes, I remember that guy," Thomas said of Frank Waters. "We told him so many things. . . ." He laughed. "But we made them all up and now they sell that book in drug stores and supermarkets, and bahanas buy it and believe it. Ha ha ha ha ha. This is how the elders protect the Hopi way."

"Bahana" is the Hopi way of calling white folks honkies.

Hearing this, I opted to learn the Hopi crafts. In a daring camp switch, I moved over to the home of one of Elizabeth's relatives. It seemed like a faux pas to refer to her as one of Thomas's relatives too, as they hadn't spoken in twenty years. Like Elizabeth, she was also a Christian and did beautiful work in Hopi basketry.

My new hostess, "Grandma," was about eighty, and she spoke only a small amount of English. Immediately upon my arrival, she started trying to get me to read to her from a Hopi-phonetic translation of the New Testament.

On my first morning at Grandma's house, she served me the most un-Craig Claiborne breakfast of my whole life. With a smile she offered me a thin, gray gruel with gray, round things floating around in it that looked like ailing matzo balls.

"Long-time-Hopi-people eat this in morning," she assured me.

I sat down and took a spoonful.

"Uhmmm," I said, taking a deep and sensuous breath as though I was savoring the full bouquet of some fine French wine. "What is it?"

"Corn and ashes," she replied, sipping some coffee and watching me eat.

"You want some?" I offered a spoonful in her direction.

"No, no. Already had. Get up with the sun, me."

Grandma was very short. The top of her head was several inches below my shoulder.

My first job at Grandma's house was hoeing in her "fields." When I first saw them I wondered if this was an unadmitted joke. "Long-time-Hopi-people plant here," she said, giving me her standard explanation for any number of her actions: "Long-time-Hopi-people do _____ [fill in the blank for whatever she wanted done]." With broad, flat "Hopi" hoes, we got to work chopping the tough desert grass and throwing it into a pile.

"Corn will grow here," she said to no one in particular. "Rains will come."

"Today, go to Elizabeth," she said one morning, after watching me eat my obligatory bowl of what long-time-Hopi-people eat. Elizabeth was going out on a clay-gathering expedition with Jacob, a potter friend of mine who was staying with her. For the past week they had been engaging in a John Henry-type competition between him on the potter's wheel versus her hand-coiling. She was ahead, naturally, but now they had run out of clay.

We piled into Jacob's truck and roared off into the Painted Desert. There were huge, dry, clay mountains on all sides of us, with many colors to choose from. We had traveled a long time when Elizabeth suddenly said *"Stop!"* Jacob slammed on the brakes, causing the people in the back of the truck to fall on their asses.

Elizabeth—because she had traveled and read widely— could not use Grandma's effective manipulation style in its exact form, but in years of dealing with bahanas she had managed to develop her own equally effective style.

We climbed out of the pickup and followed her, carrying washtubs for the clay in a reverent manner, down, down, down into a dry creek bed.

"You must eat clay," she said. "That is our secret. You can tell if it is good by the taste."

She offered a handful of dry dirt to Jacob, which he cautiously touched with his tongue.

"See? Eat some more."

When the entire handful was gone, she said, "Now that's *not* good clay," and we climbed, lugging the washtubs, out of the steep canyon.

Once the proper clay was found, we dug up a lot of it. When Elizabeth and Jacob returned to her house, they wet it down with a hose, strained it through a wire screen, and were, immediately, back at battle.

After another week, I started to feel very uncomfortable. Even in the very lofty interest of anthropology, I felt I simply could not do another thing that long-time-Hopi-people do. So I decided to leave, cutting short my stay.

"Oh, bad," Grandma said, and then with a laughing "Bye" she returned to her house, dusting off her hands.

As I was riding south back to Verde Valley School, I thought Elizabeth and Grandma should get together with Thomas, who had so delighted in fooling Frank Waters about Hopi myths and legends. They were each doing the same thing, each keeping up their ancestral heritage, guarding their own fronts. With remarkable success they were getting rid of all intruders, just as the Hopi had once kicked the Navaho from the walls of their mesa. Perhaps they were in cahoots already.

Thomas and Elizabeth, for all their family fighting, seemed to share a distinct cultural personality that I imagine must have been woven into the character of every Hopi throughout their whole long history. When I got back to school I started wondering if there were any similar threads that bonded me to the other people in *my* world. America, itself, the "melting pot," did not seem to have one unifying cultural experience of her own. I thought that if there was any group of people with whom I shared a distinct set of formative experiences, it must be my generation.

After the field trips, the school went on a recess for spring vacation. As it happened, this exactly coincided with the May Day demonstration against the war in Vietnam. After spending a few days of my vacation at home with my mother in her New York City apartment, I went down to Washington to participate in May Day. At this vast gathering of people primarily from my generation, I had a chance to consider what, if anything, I had in common with all of them.

Since it was springtime, people were wearing bright colors and many were sporting the first short sleeves of the season. The mood seemed light. At a big demonstration like this, I always saw at least seventy-five people I knew. A pleasant, warm breeze was blowing. As I walked around the Capitol grounds I came across many people I wanted to talk with to get the news from all corners of the country. Here and there I'd stop to chat, lying down beneath the Monument on the fragile, light-green spring grass.

The main news was that hardly anyone was doing the same thing that they'd been up to when I last saw them. Raymond Mungo and the hardcore staff of the radical "Liberation News Service" had made a permanent home out of an old Vermont farm. No more teletype for them. An old speed freak I knew was "so high on macrobiotics, man." David, my two-years-ago summer love, had given up political thinking in favor of listening for "the music of the spheres." A radical lesbian liberationist was now baking bread in a yoga commune. A camp counselor had joined the Hare Krishnas. These were only a few stories from all the friends I spoke with. All of them had their own trip, but generally the word, throughout the whole generation was: Get into your own head. You could almost hear sitar music floating dreamily through the cherry blossoms.

In my own way I was doing exactly the same thing. Now, in 1971, I, too, was apparently in a completely different bag than the year before. Then I was a yippie with a traveling act, intent on changing the world with theater. I was fasting for Biafra, organizing demonstrations. But there was no longer this intense activism in my life. Now, at fifteen, I was trying to understand my own spiritual nature. I was racing tumbleweeds in the desert and seeing new colors. I was working at self-discipline—not so that I could become a fearless revolutionary, but so that I could use my mind to reach ever-larger spaces of awareness.

So what had happened to us all? Had our social conscience disappeared? I talked at length with many friends to try and find out what it was that was touching all of us and moving us from political to spiritual concerns. As we spoke together, I began to see that there was a basic and profound realization at the root of our change.

Political change essentially means a change in the system of laws. But even a perfect set of laws will not make a perfect society. First of all, people at their present level of consciousness probably couldn't invent a perfect set of laws, and if they could, this perfect set of laws, once invented, would not be adhered to.

A good example of this problem is the waste of natural resources. There are many laws to limit pollution, yet they do not get to the root of the problem. Why are General Electric and other appliance manufacturers able to stay in business selling electric can openers, electric toothbrushes, TV remote control devices, and other ridiculous things? Why can Con Ed get away with the claim that they need to build more and more power plants so that they can meet the ever-increasing power needs of the American public?

There is one answer. People want these appliances and the power that runs them. At the cost of the rest of the earth, they *want* the "better and better" life offered by these appliances and this power.

Laws against pollution don't change the greed these wants reflect. Some people believe that it is *advertising,* not want, that motivates people to buy these low-usefulness products. To this I can only respond that there must be a big "something" within most people which is touched by the advertising—otherwise, it would be ineffective.

When I realized I had an "American Legion outpost" in my own head, I understood that the place to begin any kind of social change was within myself. I could no longer complain with righteousness that the reactionary forces in this country were causing all the problems. In my own tiny way, I was a reactionary force, too. But my conservatism had its positive side, too.

"Finally," I thought, "a reactionary I can do something about."

Leaving Washington, I felt happy and warm to know that I was still going in a common direction with the friends I had been involved with politically in the past few years. Though I knew I probably wouldn't see them again for a long time, I believed my cosmic gang would hang together. We didn't need a journal or a newsletter to keep up with one another's changing awareness—all each one of us had to do was follow our natural inclinations and everyone would always be *au courant.*

For the last days of my vacation I went down to Baltimore to visit my grandmother. She was now past eighty, and I wanted to see her. As I walked to the railway station in the earliest part of the morning, I thought about how history works. In Washington with my friends, I had seen clearly that there were distinct forces working in our hearts, stirring us into action. Like tiny time pills, the forces seemed to have a schedule. I wondered, what was the effect of time on the accumulation of human activities?

When I arrived in the station I was alone except for a few

people without homes, asleep on the benches. I noticed an old stairway and its handrail, which must have been built at the same time as the old Washington station. In my mind I asked it, "You have seen a lot of traffic, perhaps you can give me an answer to my questions about history."

I started down the stairs, noticing each worn place as my hands touched the metal and my feet touched the stone. I thought of a century's worth of people coming down the stairs: Some slowly, trudging with heavy packages. Children skipping ahead of young fathers with pounding feet. Young women walking with light steps. Awkward people falling. All of a sudden I started to hear them all. Quietly at first the rhythms of their steps came, and then louder and louder, till the whole high-ceilinged station should have shook with the sound. I listened to all the variations blended into one, and then it began to fade, as if the rumble had run its course, revealed its whole history, and was now joined into the present. Soon it was still, and there was just clip-clop, one set of steps. Me, walking in the empty station.

This experience satisfied me in some non-rational way. As I rode the short distance to Baltimore, I felt good. Everything was in place. Things had a beginning, a moment in the present, and then they passed on and somehow became worn into the fabric of time.

When I got to Baltimore, I had another unusual and direct experience with the processes of history. I came into my grandmother's bedroom. At eighty-four, she seemed so much older than a year before. When I was born she was seventy, but very vital, very active. Now her flesh was beginning to shrink, the skin on her hands stretching tight over tendons and knuckles. Two years before she had had a cataract operation. Now, with her pink-framed glasses, she looked like a child.

"Grannie, it's me," I said, drawing a chair close to the bed.

Her eyes were shut, so her hand stretched out to find me.

"Gladys," she called, without looking up.

"It's Sophia," I said softly, thinking she was referring to my mother, Gladys, who was in New York.

"How long since Chicago?" she asked. "Have I slept the whole day?"

This puzzled me. I didn't know what she meant.

"It's such a long ride, days and days on the train, but I love the mountains," she continued.

I sniffed in the air and thought I caught a whiff of linden flowers, the scent that provoked Proust's vivid memories in *Remembrance of Things Past*.

"Where are we going?" I whispered, hoping not to disturb her.

"To Colorado Springs," she said. "But please, Gladys, tell me, how long have we been out of Chicago?"

"I don't know. But you have been sleeping a long time. It's almost two in the afternoon."

"Mercy me, two? I met some young people last night and we got to talking. Must have been up until dawn."

Slowly I was becoming aware that my grandmother was locked into some memory and was seeing everything about it vividly, as if it were happening before her. Wishing to share her past with her as I now shared the present, I quietly asked, "Whom did you meet?"

"Gladys, it was so nice."

I now realized that Gladys was my Great-aunt Gladys, my grandmother's sister who had often traveled to Colorado Springs because the air there was better for her health.

"They both had been to the Sorbonne at the same time I was there, and with them was a young man. A most ambitious young man, too, I must say. He wanted to build a city up north of Denver, at the foot of a canyon."

That's where Boulder is, I thought, and it was founded about that time. I realized my grandmother was giving me a rare chance to see directly how history forms and my only chance to live in the Victorian era.

"He had Cripple Creek money. A friend of Winfield Stratton, or so he said. But all he did was complain about the strikers." (Miners in Colorado were just beginning to use collective bargaining in the early 1900s.)

Winfield Stratton. I repeated the name over to myself, trying to remember it. I later found out that he was a miner who had one of the original stakes in the Cripple Creek gold.

"He had nice clothes. From Paris, it's likely. But still, even though he had all that gold, it wasn't old gold, if you know what I mean. It's no wonder he had trouble with the hired help. The nouveau riche just don't know what to do with servants."

"Can we go meet them now? Are they around?" I asked. I wanted to meet some of Grannie's friends. This crack in history was remarkable enough, but I wanted to understand it better. I wondered if my grandmother and I could cause the characters to turn and see us across all of the years; to pause from the activities which they had been repeating over and over since their deaths, at least in the minds of the people who knew them, and speak to us in the living present.

"All right." She smiled, her eyes still closed. "But let me get dressed. These are *General Palmer's daughters*." (General Palmer was the founder and leading citizen of Colorado Springs.)

My grandmother seemed to sleep a half hour or so and then she woke and called out, "Gladys, I'm ready to go."

"Can you introduce me?" I asked.

My grandmother paused a moment and then her face became puzzled. "How strange," she said slowly. "They looked as if they heard me speak, because they turned and looked, but then when their gazes scanned the room, they passed right over me."

Grannie's voice trailed off. With the puzzled look on her face, she once again fell asleep.

CHAPTER
5

"CAN I GET SOMETHING FOR YOU, MISS SOPHIA?"

I looked up from the book I was reading. It was one of my grandmother's leather-bound volumes of the Dialogues of Plato. I was just at the sad place where Socrates is lying in prison, about to drink hemlock and end his life.

"Orange juice, please," I replied to Sita, my grandmother's new live-in servant.

It was about two months since I had last been in Baltimore. In the time that had passed I had finished up the tenth grade at Verde Valley School and secured permission to skip the eleventh grade by going to summer school. I had decided to go to school in Baltimore, though I chose it not so much for the school or because my family was there, as for an interesting job I had found working in a hospital pathology and blood lab.

Certain that this next year was going to be my last year in high school, I had begun to mull over what I was going to do in the year after next year, and then after that and after that. I thought it was appropriate to have at least some plans to present to the "Whitridge-Collier Foundation" (my parents) when I went to ask for funding for my next four years. I assumed those next four years would be spent at college, and I was now trying on the idea of becoming a medical doctor.

Medicine. The word itself should be accompanied by trumpets when it comes out of the mouth of a young person considering it as a vocation. Even today, people think of it as such a clean and respectable thing. I imagined so many parents telling their kids who went "clean for Gene" in '68: "Son, you want to help the world? You want to relieve human suffering? Become a doctor."

And when a young person going into Medicine (did you hear the trumpets?) does everything right, at the end of his life he's rich—rightly rewarded for all of his earnest care for his fellow man.

When I mentioned my interest in medicine to some of my Baltimore relatives, they hauled out the family album and pointed to a great-great-uncle of mine, Grover Perin, a model of sobriety, who had been the Surgeon General.

Medicine had many things to recommend it. But what was it really like? In the job I had found in the hospital lab, I thought I could get a look into the back rooms of the profession and find out how doctors really felt about their work. My job was a general all-around flunky. Quite a way from Surgeon General, but you had to start someplace.

Sita came back with the orange juice—wonderfully cold, fresh-squeezed stuff in a tall glass on a silver coaster.

"Ahhh." I breathed deeply and felt happy. Bach was playing on the speakers, Horowitz at piano. He was one of my grandmother's few Jewish heroes. The air in the living room was cool. It always seemed to be the same temperature no matter how hot it got outside. I didn't plan to stay at Grannie's while I was in Baltimore. Instead, I had rented a place in a poorer part of town. After a while, being at my grandmother's house got to be too much. All that "Miss Sophia" stuff embarrassed me. I didn't see any reason for people to be running around waiting on me, yet if I went in the kitchen to get something for myself that too created an uncomfortable situation. It was interpreted to mean that I felt the servants weren't good enough to get whatever it was I wanted.

When my mother was a few years older than I was now, she had felt a similar urgency about leaving the Baltimore social environment. When she graduated from Bryn Mawr, she couldn't move to New York fast enough. In New York she lived in Greenwich Village, where she met my father, who at the time was making his living as an artist.

I had been at Grannie's a few days when I got a phone call from Eliot. Without even telling me, my Verde Valley School sweetheart had started hitchhiking across the country to see me. He was calling from a little town in Pennsylvania. Like me, Eliot had ancestral roots in Baltimore. Later we figured out that it was very possible our relatives had known each other (perhaps they had even chatted over lunch at the Maryland Club) a hundred years before. Eliot's Baltimore connection was his father, the popular historian, Page Smith. When that side of the family wanted to get out of Baltimore, they went farther than New York—all the way to Santa Cruz, California.

I was delighted to have Eliot as my summertime companion, because I was already feeling a little lonely. When Eliot arrived he had his knapsack on his back and a very long list of every town he'd been through on his journey. The rides had taken him seven days, because he was not yet a true stalwart hitchhiker who thumbed both day and night.

While I was busy-busy-busy with school and work, Eliot stayed home and read science fiction books, wrote poetry, and drank Kool-Aid, a drink I could not wean him from, even with all my tirades on health foods.

Things at school went well. Though my math class did not afford me any lasting insights into the "beauty bare," with some success I learned a bit about geometry. At the hospital lab things were a little dull. The day proceeded from task to task in an expected way. All interest and intrigue had to be supplied by my own imagination. One day while I was all alone watching the lab machines, it occurred to me that each one of them had a particular character, like a musical instrument. Soon I found myself "conducting" an imaginary symphony of their various sounds, using a thermometer for a baton. I imagined the spectrograph to have high, clavichord-like trills; the centrifuge made low, long sounds like a timpani. By the end of the summer I was beginning to get the idea that being a doctor might not be the profession for me—though I didn't give up the notion entirely for another few years.

Toward the end of the summer, Eliot went home to California, leaving me to finish up my business in Baltimore. In the middle of August, school and job done, I decided to spend the rest of the summer traveling around visiting my scattered pals. One of the advantages of being a boarding school scholar is that you know people from many parts of the country. Your best friends, most likely, are from areas hundreds of miles apart. As an independent and adventurous fifteen-year-old, this seemed like a prime chance to see the world without joining the Navy.

I got on a plane and went first to Arizona and then to California, arriving in Los Angeles. After I had been in L.A. a few days, I began hitchhiking up the coast. I stopped in Malibu to see a schoolmate whose father was a Hollywood producer; then I was on my way to Santa Cruz to see Eliot, by way of Big Sur. I planned to camp with some other friends whom I would meet there. It was a rather casual arrangement. By the time I reached Big Sur, I had met some sweet Jesus Freaks and was traveling with them. By midnight I felt too tired to continue on, so I parted ways with them to camp down for the night.

However, I made a very unfortunate choice of camps. The other people at the campsite were in no mood to sleep, but instead were intent on drinking themselves into a frenzy. Realizing the situation, I was scared and wanted to get out of there fast. Wearily, I climbed back into my boots and walked back to the road all alone, hitching in the lonely ponderosas of Big Sur. The night was beautiful in a haunting way. The moon was almost full and covered slightly by clouds. After a time, a pickup truck slowed and stopped. I ran with my duffle bag and climbed in. The man seemed friendly, and without conversation we drove up Route 1 through the night.

Then, without a word, the man stopped the truck.

"Just a minute," he said, and went and stood behind the truck. I figured he was urinating. When he got back in the truck his fly was down and his penis was exposed. On his face was a very hard look. I grabbed the door handle and pushed to get out of the truck. The door was stuck. When I managed to push it open, the man had come around to my side of the truck.

"You don't want to have anything to do with me," I said. "I have VD." I lied, hoping the thought of getting VD would cool him off.

"You little bitch," he said, with further obscenities. Clenching his teeth, he pushed me up against the cab, and through my mind flashed the thought, "My mother always told me this would happen." A car went by and I screamed *Help, Help, Help*. I heard it echo off into the night as the red taillights of the car passed at sixty miles an hour. The man pushed me harder. He raised his fist to my face.

"I didn't want to have to hurt you, but now I am going to have to kill you," he hissed through his pursed mouth. "I'm going to knock you cold."

I saw he meant it. And I saw myself lying dead in the grass. More than anything I wanted to live. In that instant I felt so full of love for being alive. I felt powerfully connected to the life force that pushes grass up through cement and has made life endure against great obstacles since time began.

A deep and tremendous calm came over me. I looked into the man's eyes and said with all the love I had for life, "You know, it's really all right, things are going to be all right." The hardness in his face melted and his fist relaxed.

"I want to make love," he said, as if he was begging. I felt so much pity for him.

"Okay," I said, seeing this was my only way to continue living.

I tried to make it a nice experience for him. I felt a genuine sense of compassion. But when he got up off me, my mind was working, thinking how I could turn him in to the police.

"My name is Sophia," I said, managing a smile.

"Lee," he said, as if he was ashamed.

"I'm a Pisces. I love the ocean." I tried to start a conversation. He was a Pisces also.

"You never know the violence inside," he said. "I've never lost control like this before. I'm sorry. I'm sorry. I'm sorry." We walked back to his truck. He was crying a little.

"Can I take you to Monterey?" he wanted to know.

"Do you live there?" I asked, gathering evidence about his identity.

"Yes."

We rode to Monterey, and when he let me off he helped me with my stuff.

"In another circumstance you might have liked me," he said. As he drove away at the highway exit to his home, I wrote down the license plate number.

I walked down the exit ramp to an all-night cafeteria. A mother and daughter were walking out of the place. I went up to them and said I'd just been raped. They both put their arms around me and, at last feeling safe, my composure collapsed and I started to sob. They called the police and some officers took me to the station. Everyone there was very kind. The police picked up the man right away and I identified him from a lineup. He was a local family man and had a daughter my age.

I called my folks and spoke to my father. From him I received a tremendous infusion of love and support. I signed some statements and was taken to the county hospital. There I was examined by a female doctor, one of the toughest and most butch women I have ever met.

"So, sweetie, what happened to you?" she said, as she conducted the pelvic examination.

Tired beyond anything I had ever experienced, I said, "I was raped," in an impatient and rude tone.

"Did you know the man?" she said, roughly scraping my cervix for a semen sample, and going on to imply that all sex with men was rape.

"Hell, no, I didn't know the man," I said, and tried, through my tiredness, to speak in defense of men.

She raised her eyebrows and looked at me with contempt.

From the county hospital a matron drove me to JD hall, where I was put in a little cell because I was a suspected runaway. There I fell into a grateful sleep. It took about three days for my parents to convince the California authorities that I hadn't run away from home.

When I got out of JD hall, I spent a day in San Francisco. It was a cool and windy afternoon, the kind that reminds you that summer is ending and autumn is on the way. Brown leaves blew on the sidewalk, fallen from trees still mostly full of green. I walked up and down the hills and felt melancholy. After a while I bought an apple, sat on a sidewalk bench and did my first real reflecting on my recent experiences. Mostly I had a feeling of sympathy and sorrow for the suffering man who had attacked me, and the bitter doctor at the hospital. In front of my eyes, I had seen the man's hate and violence dissolve into a whimpering for love and warmth.

I finished the apple and ate the whole core, seeds and all. I thought about sex. That such a thing would have ever been invented was an amazement in itself to me. If you think about it from a detached perspective, as if you were a person from Mars who had never participated in any sexual activity, it seems like a rather unlikely thing for people to do together. Orgasm seems like even more of a surprise.

Not all of my previous sexual experiences had been pleasant, but when Eliot and I made love it was a very tender and moving experience. I loved it, and I hoped this most recent experience would not somehow hurt my future intimacies.

A few hours later I was on a jet going home. My mother met me at the airport and we drove to East Hampton. She asked me what had happened and how it made me feel. I told her the whole story and then added, "But I wasn't a virgin, so . . ."

This was the first time we had really talked about my sex life. The only other time we had broached the subject was a year before when we were driving on the Long Island Expressway and I asked her if she enjoyed sex. The question caught her so unaware, that, the way she tells the story, she made a wrong turn and, next thing she knew she was driving on the Cross Bronx Expressway, headed for New England. If you know the roads on Long Island, you know that this is a very difficult wrong turn to make, as the Expressway is in no way contiguous with the Cross Bronx. At any rate we were silent for the rest of the three-hour drive.

When I talked to my father about sex it was much more open. A year later, when I was almost sixteen, I told him I was taking birth control pills. His only question was, "Do they work?"

"I think so," I said.

And so the summer ended and I went back to Verde Valley School.

Note: When the case went to trial, I was called as a witness and testified for six hours in front of the jury on two occasions. The man was found innocent of all charges, including statutory rape.

His defense was that I had consented to have sex with him in exchange for a ride; then, after he felt too tired to take me any farther than his hometown, I became angry and went to the police out of a mix of wanting revenge and being upset over having sex with a man so much older than me.

I guess this was an easy story for a middle-aged, hippie-weary California jury to believe.

CHAPTER

6

I WAS VERY SURPRISED TO FIND MYSELF HUMMING AS I UN-packed my clothes on the first day of the '71–'72 school year at Verde Valley. I thought, Me? Ace hater of school, humming happily in the face of another nine months? Incredible. The year before, it had been only the fear of the truant officer hunting me down at the swimming hole that had finally convinced me to unpack at all. And now, at fifteen, I was actually enjoying the thought of the coming year. Maybe I was growing up, I thought; everyone told me it would happen.

Outside my window I heard the sounds of other students unpacking. Lots of laughing. Trucks pulling in and out with luggage. The moans and thuds of skinny students carrying trunks too heavy for them to bear. After a while, on that first day back at school, I ran downstairs and caught a ride with Verde Valley's down-home headmaster, who was making baggage runs on a tractor.

"Hey, Sophia," was the first thing I heard when I got into the center of the campus. I jumped off the tractor and went over to receive a hug from my old pal, Ellen. Ellen and I looked incredibly alike. From the back, people would often mistake us for each other. Soon we were immersed in gossip and chatter about old students who would not be returning to school this year and the new kids who would be replacing them.

"Did you know Annie Lockhart's little sister is coming to school this year?" Ellen asked, referring to a dormmate, the daughter of actress June Lockhart.

"Yeah, I hope she can draw as well as Annie. She did that front piece in *Ambro* last year."

Ambro was the literary magazine of which I was editor.

"No, she wants to be an actress, but she's fat."

"So what about character parts? Listen, Eliot's father sold his book."

"Oh? You mean the two-part history of the Revolutionary War?"

"Right. They are going to do it for the Bicentennial."

"Bicentennial?" Ellen was incredulous. "Do you think there is going to *be* any Bicentennial?"

I shrugged my shoulders. It was sad to think things in America would be so much the same in '76 as in '71 that a publisher could already be comfortably planning their sales campaign five years in advance. After a few hours, helloes all done, I decided to go off and reacquaint myself with my biggest best friend from the year before: the desert.

When I got out beyond the school fence, I was so happy to see the red dirt. I wondered if the tumbleweed would be waiting, ready to race, or if a skunk I'd once met would be poised to spray. I climbed up one of the huge red-rock mountains. It was the same one on which I had stood a year before and taken stock of Verde Valley for the first time. A breeze was blowing. It was warm, but it definitely had autumn in it. Far in the distance, I saw the creek where I'd camped the year before. On it edges grew cottonwood trees, whose leaves get yellow like aspens with the autumn's shorter days.

Here I was back at school, and I was a senior too. I could hardly believe it. This was my last year. What had I learned, at this grand old age of fifteen? Thinking this made me smile and laugh out loud, as I remembered Holden Caulfield, J. D. Salinger's hero in *Catcher in the Rye*. Holden had considered the question many times, thinking about his class visits to the Museum of Natural History in New York. He'd decided that each time he'd come to the museum he was different in some way. It wasn't that he was older or wiser. He was just different, "because I'd seen a rainbow or an oilslick or something like that," and it had changed him in some definite but undefined way.

So, me? What had I seen? What was different about me? There is a kind of analysis I might call "Other People's Parents." It has to do with the superficial and quicker-than-a-wink synopsis of your life and aims that you stammer out between jam and toast at breakfast on the first morning of a stay at the home of a school chum.

Under this quick scrutiny, you try to look good. Not so much for your own sake, but for the sake of your friend, who will be regarded with greater esteem in her or his family if she or he has the credit of keeping the companionship of good kids. You, by what you present of yourself, want to assure the parents that you are *not* a doper, ne'er-do-well, or junior crook who will in no time be leading their child down the road to ruin.

From the point of view of other people's parents, I was doing fine.

"Fifteen years old and a senior in high school. Wants to be a doctor, my, my." And then, between jam and toast, the other people's parents smile and start speaking directly to you, as if their son or daughter were not in the room. "Janie doesn't really know what she wants to do. But she's very smart. I recommend college, but she's not sure. What do you think?"

This is always an uncomfortable moment, begging for a tactful escape.

"Oh, yes," I say, "Janie's been a good friend to me. She's very sensitive, I'm sure she'll make the right choice. Can you please put in another piece of toast for me?"

So much for other people's parents. In *my* opinion, my little life so far was anything but a success. I felt I hadn't

even grasped the basics. I didn't know something as funda-
mental and simply put as "the meaning and purpose of life."
This working familiarity with why we are alive seemed to
me to be a prerequisite to all other endeavors. Without understanding this one point, it seemed foolish for me to go
ahead with anything else.

The sun was beginning to go down. I made my way down
the mountain and back to my dorm room. There I found my
new roommate, bidding her last passionate good-byes to her
boyfriend, a motorcyclist fifteen years her senior. After he
left, she began what turned out to be her every-evening pre-
occupation—fulminations over whether she should run away
from school and marry him. In a month she finally made up
her mind: she left the school in the dead of night, and left
me with our huge room all to myself.

I filled my first nights more conventionally—with homework. This year I had signed up for classes like French,
trigonometry, and similar staples of the senior's diet. Every
day I faithfully went to class and avoided getting sidetracked,
as had happened to me so many times the previous year.

Sitting down to do my homework, I soon discovered that
something remarkable had happened to me. Somehow I had
developed a very strong ability to concentrate. I could focus
my mind with such intensity that I found I could read several pages with almost total recall in an hour's time, without
skimming. Sometimes I felt that my mind was a large com-
puter which I was watching in operation, feeding it energy
to work but doing none of the work myself.

Why I experienced at this time this tremendously height-
ened ability to concentrate I cannot even guess. As my friend
who sends me *The New York Times* says: "To play cause
and effect, you have to know all the causes and all the effects.
Only then can you sort out the 'why' of things." Forgetting
this in a moment of spiritual pride, I decided that the
reason I could concentrate so well was due solely to my
meager efforts at disciplining my mind. My austerity pro-

gram begun the year before was bearing some fruit. Later, free from hubris, I just attributed it to luck and tried to take advantage of it while it was with me. And sure enough, just like luck, as surprisingly as this enhanced concentration appeared in that autumn of 1971, it was gone by the springtime of 1972. These days my mind would concentrate much like anyone else's: When put to work, it rebels immediately and becomes full of flighty thoughts, itches, fidgets, and ideas of other projects (that letter to Danielle?) that I should be undertaking now, instead of the work which I have in front of me.

In October I started writing away for college applications, although, without an understanding of the purpose and meaning of life, I felt it was ridiculous to go ahead with anything. Still, with the passage of time I was becoming swept along from class to class, day to day, into college and into life. I felt that my circumstances, rather than my true wishes for myself, were beginning to take hold of my future. This became an overriding thought, made more plain and urgent with each passing day.

Inge, my friend who had helped me get out of classes the year before, taught one of my English classes. One day I was going down to her house to consult with her about some schoolwork. Arriving at her door, I found it ajar, though it was dark inside. From the bedroom I heard the muffled sound of crying. I tiptoed in, not knowing if I could help or not. I had heard she was having some personal difficulties. When I got inside the bedroom, I saw her alone on the bed, her body shaking with sobs. I went over to her and put my hand on her back. Since she didn't seem to notice me, I spoke softly to her. She turned over slightly and looked up. Her expression was one of suffering and hurt. Her wrinkled face was red and swollen and her eyes were like a weeping child's. Right away I began to cry too. I felt as though I had encountered the whole sum of human life in her: the noble-

ness of her sixty years reduced to a terrible pain and suffering.

I was immediately reminded of one of the only times I saw
my father cry. I was about ten; we had gone to see a film
about the life of Isadora Duncan, the innovator of modern
dance. In the middle of it, my father took my hand and led
me from the theater. When we reached the car he sat down,
rested his head on the steering wheel, and began to cry.

"It all came to nothing," he said several times, sobbing.

Then, remembering me, he explained. First, Isadora Duncan's children were killed in an auto accident and then, in
the still-fullness of her own life, she was killed, choked by
her own scarf which had caught in the wheel of her car.
Hearing how this beautiful and unusually free and creative
life was ended in such a cruel way made me cry too, with
my father.

I looked again into Inge's eyes.

"Leave me," she said. "Please go."

"But, but . . ." I wanted to tell her something that would
comfort her, tell her that I loved her, that she was one of the
finest people I knew; but she pressed again.

"I'll see you tomorrow," she said kindly, as if speaking to
a child, and trying to hide the grim truth of adult life.

The college applications started to come in, and they piled
up on my desk, waiting to be filled out. There they were:
Radcliffe, Bryn Mawr, Wesleyan—all fine schools. I felt confident that at least one of them would take me. I had even
sent away for an application to Southampton College, a little
place near where my mother lives, thinking it might be nice
to live at home for a change.

As the days passed, though I continued to excel at my
schoolwork, my disquiet grew. It was evident to everyone.
One day I was walking through the main part of the campus,
thinking terrifically hard about the nature of life, when the
headmaster's wife, Melinda, came up to me.

"You have an expression that nobody your age should have," she said. "What is it that troubles you?"

"Melinda, I don't know the meaning of life. And I don't know anyone who can tell me. I look at New York City and all the cities in the country and everybody's got some scene, some trip they're trying to do, but why? For what purpose? If there is no point to life, I don't want to slave and sweat, follow everybody's foolish morality, just to go nowhere. I don't want to become a big shot just to drop dead and rot in the ground. If that's all there is to life, I sometimes feel, damn it, why not just drop dead now."

Melinda looked at me for a long time, as if she was trying to think of something to say by way of consolation.

"Oh, Melinda," I sighed, "please don't worry about me."

"I wasn't," she said. "I was worrying about myself, my own soul."

As William James said, the still and sad parts of life seem to come from a deeper region and strike us with appalling convincingness. But despite this persuasiveness, I continued to believe that joy, not sorrow, was at the base of life. I had a faith that there was a marvelous destiny for human life *and that I would discover it*. After all, I had been on the inside of that East Hampton wave. I knew, deep inside me, that there was something, an inexplicable "something" going on in the world that was beyond all sorrow, and that I, as sure as Buddha had, would know it. I could not stay depressed for too long.

It was January, 1972. The morning was cool but sunny. Walking to breakfast I smelled something new in the air. Sniff. What is that, apart from all the scents of toast and eggs cooking in the kitchen, apart from the coffee brewing and the strong, sweet smell of straw that drifted down from the stables? Sniff. It smells like snow. By mid-morning clouds were in the sky. They came rolling down the mountains from Flagstaff, full and deep gray. The sun shone through them for an hour or so, making the ground an eerie twilight color with its gray-yellow light. Then the first flakes fell, cold and wet on the Arizona desert.

It was such an unusual thing. Everyone poured out of the classrooms and ran around in shirtsleeves, faces upturned. Some people, the younger and less inhibited, opened their mouths with their tongues sticking out, darting back and forth to catch and crunch that one special flake they saw falling. Then the snow fell harder, sticking to the ground. Soon there was enough to make snowballs out of. Fights broke out. The whole area was covered with a marvelous, sparkling white. The red rocks held the snow only in patches. Since they had stood for months in the open sun, they had stored heat which melted away the white snow and left the rock stained a deeper red in its wetness.

In another hour the sun was breaking through again. The clouds which had seemed so gray and thick were evaporating into the upper sky. The snow began to melt; the air became warm; the green of the desert was perked up from the water which still sat in droplets on the leaves. And such a surprise —birds began to sing. We had seen the gathering of the autumn, the deep winter, and the coming of the spring all in one day. With such a brilliant display of playfulness and profound beauty, how could I doubt that all life was rooted in joy?

The next day I felt good. I took up all the college applications and threw them in the trash. All except for the one little school near my mother's home. That one I filled out with great care and sent off. In a week they wrote back saying I was accepted.

It was during this period of exuberance and college plans that I invented the Do-It-Yourself University.

CHAPTER
7

THE DO-IT-YOURSELF UNIVERSITY WAS BASICALLY A SCIENCE school. It was founded on this tenet: A human being is a self-contained laboratory. Inside of each person are some of the finest examples of biological, chemical, and physical principles that can be found anywhere. What's more, each human being's mental functioning provides a case history through which it is possible to study sociology, psychology and the other behavioral sciences. The classroom for the Do-It-Yourself University was a dark closet. The lesson plan was intense thought.

Initially I was the only student at the school. Then gradually, as I spoke to other people about the Do-It-Yourself idea, the number of students grew to eight, all of them setting up solitary classrooms in their own dark closets. Occasionally we swapped notes on our experiences and findings, but generally we kept our camaraderie quiet. Each of us was pursuing fields so diverse that one's discoveries were not of much help to another.

The first course I took at the Do-It-Yourself University was human biology. I studied for one hour a day, lying on my back and keeping my body extremely still on a soft rug in my closet classroom.

I concentrated on my breath and let all thoughts fade from mind. I was accustomed, as I imagine most people are, to feeling mostly on the surface of my body. Generally, I paid the most attention to sensations of heat, cold, texture, and other feelings that created the changes on the surface of my skin. I was only aware of the sensations inside my body as signs of some internal lack of balance, like hunger, a sore throat, or a pulled muscle. Lying on the floor of my closet, I wanted to learn to feel my body at rest, to experience the normal tone of internal functions.

Not knowing where to begin, I just lay still and concentrated on the aliveness in me. Soon I felt this quality of aliveness was particularly apparent in the circulation of my blood. I became aware of the pulsebeats at various points in my body. For the first few lessons the only thing I did was to listen to these pulses. Their continuous rhythm moved from the stillest, most gentle touches of pulse in the remote capillary beds to the thunderously loud, powerful beat of my heart. In a week's time I was familiar with the path of my circulation through its whole long journey. My body seemed like a five-pointed star, with my heart in the center and the blood flowing out into each of the points, my two legs, two arms, and head.

After examining the route my blood took in my body, I tried to isolate a sensation on the inside of my blood vessels. Surely, with all that warm fluid passing on the inside of the veins and arteries, they felt something. I wanted to bring that feeling into my consciousness.

In another week I found I could concentrate on any area of my body and locate particular sensations within my blood vessels. Having isolated these sensations, I found I could determine the direction of the blood flowing inside any individual vessel. To practice this newfound skill I chose a place in my body and followed a particular part of my bloodstream through its course back to my heart. As I traveled within my own body, I explored the feelings of the insides of the hollow tubes of vessels. By carefully concentrating on where they were and where they weren't, I developed a mental picture of their shapes and irregularities. When the blood reached my heart, I followed it through the heart's soft curves and valves. I spent a long time concentrating on the inside of my heart and wondering why it was built in the shape it seemed to be. Fascinated by these questions of biological architecture, I looked in *Gray's Anatomy* to find a picture of the human heart. The illustrator's rendering of the heart's interior shape was very similar to what I had visualized.

With renewed confidence, I continued to study my insides in this same manner of isolating internal feelings. Eventually I moved on from circulation to digestion, where I familiarized myself with the passages and workings of my alimentary canal. I was very happy with the success of the Do-It-Yourself University and wondered why this sort of approach was not more commonplace in schools and colleges. Experiencing things firsthand seems like the best way to learn.

One day, while the Do-It-Yourself University was in full swing, a young man from the little community where Jess's cabin was appeared at Verde Valley School. In the course of his stay on campus he heard of the Do-It-Yourself University. Believing himself to be of great spiritual attainment, he volunteered to teach at the Do-It-Yourself University. After a hasty meeting of the board, we decided such a thing was out of the question.

"A *teacher* at the Do-It-Yourself University? Unheard of!"

Though we had nothing against teachers, the idea of the institution was clearly Do-It-Yourself. The "It" here refers to the primary revelation of a new piece of knowledge. When "it" is done for you, then you take on a passive role. You have to trust the experts and memorize their findings. There is something unattractive about this dependency and it summed up my feelings about teachers and gurus in general: I wasn't into them. Don Juan was fine for Carlos Castaneda. Guru Maharaj Ji was fine for Baba Ram Dass. But me? I was the kind of person who, had I been a man of another socio-economic bracket, would have been building a red-wood patio in my backyard from plans I had found in *Popular Science* magazine. Clearly, I was a do-it-yourselfer.

At this time my life took a surprising turn, which began with a dream I had one night in the late winter. I awakened with a start, covered with sweat. Immediately I remembered my dream. I had been walking through an unfamiliar town when I came upon a house. I was full of an urge to enter, but people on the street cautioned me not to go in. Seeing no danger, I left the crowd behind and pushed open the door. On a table in the first room I entered was a flute and a note that said, "happy." Somehow I deduced from this that there was a little boy who lived here and he was happy beyond any worldly way. "Like little Krishna," I thought, remembering the Hindu God-incarnate figure who played the flute.

Going off from this first room was a staircase at the top of which, I presumed, this marvelous little boy lived. After several flights, I arrived at his door. I knocked and was invited in. The little boy, who was about nine, stood with his back to me, gazing out a large window.

The view was not the ordinary scene you might expect from the fourth story of a building. There were none of the roofs of the surrounding buildings, and no trees. Instead, there was a deep uniform field of blue that looked vast and open, like the night sky without stars. He turned and smiled, "Yes?"

"What will happen?" I stammered out, asking to know the fate of all life.

"Oh, eventual doom," he replied, not the least bit disturbed.

I was disappointed with his answer.

"I know that," I said in an impatient tone, "but will we ever get to be with God before that?"

The little boy looked serious for a moment.

"Look," he said, "first you must ask: Is there God or Is there not God? This is the most important question. Then we can talk about these other things."

He smiled again and started to fade. I awoke in a start.

"God?" I thought. "Why was I asking about God?"

I didn't believe in God.

I turned over in my bed. There was something in this dream that moved me greatly. It was haunting and would not let me sleep. This small boy had an utterly *assured* quality that I lacked. His was not the kind of confidence that lets you stand up and speak your mind in front of a crowd—I had plenty of that. On this little boy's face was an expression of transcendent happiness. He had the look from the inside of the East Hampton wave. But more than that, he was inside me. *And he wanted me to look for God.*

I didn't believe in God, though I had warmed up to the idea since the time when my "Good food, Good meat, Good God, Let's eat" speech had upset my kindergarten teacher, Miss Grimes. If there was a God, I thought of it being a conscious, loving force that was giving cohesion, on the subatomic level, to the universe. But I really didn't know, and until this midnight, I really didn't care.

"God or not," I thought, "I have to do the dishes, do my homework, do everything myself. I have had many wonderful experiences with nature and I never had to subscribe to an idea of any God to have these experiences." God or no God seemed to make little difference.

Now I realized that it did make a difference. The ineffable "meaning" I felt life needed was actually a religious wish. I now realized that the passionate concerns I had poured out to Melinda while standing in the school square, quickly and succinctly boiled down to a question about the existence of God. While I was considering these things through the night I kept remembering the little boy's face. His peace was irresistible. By dawn I had fallen asleep.

All the next day and in the days that followed, as I went

about my business, my mind was preoccupied with this question: Is there God or Is there not God? Is there God or Is there not God? I talked to many people about it and I heard the index of views. "Jesus Christ is God." "God is energy." "There are many forms of gods, and *goddesses* too." "God is foolishness, the refuge of the weak."

It was interesting to hear people talk about this subject, but other people's views offered no answer to my question. I still didn't know what to do. Someone suggested I throw myself off a cliff and then pray. If there was a God, the angels would catch me and deliver me to safety.

"But if there isn't any God . . ." I protested this jest.

"Then you'll no doubt go to hell," he replied with the same amount of wit which had prompted the suggestion.

After a week it occurred to me, why not take Revelation 101 at the Do-It-Yourself University? This would not be easy. Listening to your own heartbeat and feeling the rush of your own blood is one thing. They are physical sensations and because they have a corporeal existence, like a needle in a haystack, they can be found with some diligent effort. But trying to tune into and understand an incorporeal force was something else entirely. Looking inside yourself for God seemed like running after wind. Yet, unlike wind, God might not even exist. Besides, I thought, if God is the loving, directing force giving order and life to all things, then I am made of God. Logically, if I, part and parcel of God, go to look for God, I run smack into the Heisenberg Uncertainty Principle which explains that the act of observing inevitably changes the process under observation.

If I am made out of God and I go to look for God, how would I recognize that part of me which is God? It would be like water looking for water. These philosophic hurdles aside, I was determined to give Revelation 101 a tug. For encouragement I had the scriptures, testimonies of successful graduates. These accounts from every culture told of people who had ferreted out something they called God, confronted it, and been moved in deep and passionate ways.

The first sessions of Revelation 101 at the Do-It-Yourself University were abysmal failures; frustrating or boring efforts that showed my mind to be full, not of God, but of petty thoughts and daily concerns. Anybody who has tried meditation of any kind will sympathize with my novitiate experiences.

However, it seems whenever you really want a moral or spiritual change to come about in your life and the conscious effort you put toward it bears no fruit, your subconscious eventually takes over the work. It starts to realign the elements in your mind, so that the thoughts and attitudes which had previously obstructed your progress no longer inhibit your spiritual growth. Once your mind is free, the experience you want suddenly bursts through into your conscious mind like a revelation, like an infusion of grace.

A simple example of this is trying to remember someone's name. Often you can think really hard, trying to remember without success. But then when you relax and let your subconscious mind work on it in a more roundabout way, suddenly, in the middle of some other activity, you will remember. William James thought that if there is a God and if that God works on people at all, certainly he would work through the unconscious door of a person's perception because it is open more of the time. Whether it was God or only my strong desire at work in me, I soon had a powerful experience.

It began in the early evening. (I had recently decided that the Do-It-Yourself University was best thought of as a night school.) I was in my friend Ellen's room listening to some fine jazz records of Alice Coltrane. The music was night music, impetuous and searching. I lay back on Ellen's bed and closed my eyes. Instead of seeing the soft patterns of color that I usually do when my eyes are shut, I was aware of forms and objects that seemed quite real. In this new world I was standing in a luminous cavern, knee-deep in warm, bright, green-blue water. A little distance from me, rising out of the water, were old stone steps leading up to an oaken door, dark and brown. On the steps stood a monk in dark robes and hood. I took a step in the water and then opened my eyes again into the world of jazz and Ellen's room.

"Some music," Ellen said to me. "It really takes you to another world, huh, Soph?"

"Sure," I said, excusing myself to go sit alone in my closet classroom. Closing my eyes, I was immediately back with the monk. The air was humid and heavy with mist. The water made a haze of blue-green between us. As I watched him, he slowly opened the heavy door and beckoned me to enter the room behind it. I waded through the water and climbed the stone steps into a lighted chamber with walls and floor of fitted rock. Turning to ask where I was, I heard the sound of the door slowly shutting and locking. I was struck with a sense of finality. There was no going back now. I looked around the room. It was dry, and I thought it must be part of the lower chambers of a cathedral. At one corner of the room was a dark stairway, which I decided to go up. At the top there was a heavy trap door. I pushed it open and found I was in a great hall. In the distance, two or three hundred yards away at the far end of this room, I heard a rumbling sound, like a solemn parade.

I ran to hide, to get out of sight and watch. Cowering in a little archway behind a huge stone pillar, I peered out at the advancing crowd. People on horseback who looked like medieval crusaders led the procession. Behind them, I recognized all the popes, each with a retinue in splendor and satin. Then came the Christian saints, heads held high to be counted in that number. Finally, at the end of the line was Jesus, tagging along with his arm wrapped loosely around Saint Francis. In striking contrast to the others, the two of them were laughing and joking like prep-school boys. Around them was a herd of small white lambs.

It was the lambs that saw me first, and they all soon came over to where I was crouching. Baaaing, they pushed me with their soft heads. Jesus casually turned and said, "Hey, you're that little girl who is looking for God. Now you've got our sheep."

"Uh, oh," Saint Francis said, noticing the entire procession was turning around and heading back toward us. He looked scared, and I picked up on the cue.

"What shall I do?" I asked.

"Hide," he said with some severity.

I knelt among the sheep.

Soon the entire procession was around us. Saint Paul, dressed in ornate regalia, dismounted his horse and pointed at me.

"You have no right to be here," he said. "You are a disgusting wretch. You are full of vile human pride. Vile human desires. Vile human excrement."

"You're really one to talk," I said, somehow feeling very brave. "Look, Paul, you and your letters have screwed up the Christian Church for the last two thousand years."

Jesus laughed very softly behind me. "See Franny, she knows."

Paul mounted his horse again in a huff. Each pope in turn dismounted and rebuked me for being a human being, falling prey to human faults, and enjoying human pleasures.

"You like sex!" one shrieked in horror and disgust. "No wonder you were raped. All women are whores. You want to take men from the path of glory."

I was crying under all this abuse, but I didn't feel weak.

"You people know nothing of God. I love life. I am glad to love," I told them fiercely.

The crowd picked me up and carried me, as if to a lynching, toward the main door of the cathedral.

"Jesus, Francis, where is your father?" I yelled back to the two standing among the sheep.

The crowd pulled open the doors. Outside was the same deep blue field that the little boy in my dream had gazed at through his window.

"I'll meet you," Jesus yelled after me. The crowd threw me out the door into the vastness of space. "Get out of this garden," someone screamed as I fell into the deep. I was glad to go.

Floating in the open space, I felt my body dissolving into the blue field around me. I kept resisting, trying with all my might to keep my body together. This must be the experience of death, I thought. Finally I gave up, relaxed, and was gone, spread out a thousand miles in the sky. Somehow I still had an awareness of my existence, but I felt that I had no body, as if I had permanently and completely merged with the open nothingness of space.

Then I remembered Jesus had said, "I'll meet you."

Suddenly I felt strangely heavy. I was falling again. I landed with a thump on the ground, on the earth, facedown in the grass. Slightly in front of me, there were two brown feet in sandals. Saffron robes fell softly across them. I looked up slowly. It was a person with a smile so full of love I thought it must be him.

"Where's Franny?" I said to my sweet friend.

"Oh, back with the sheep."

We sat in the grove. Jesus picked a flower and twirled it in his hand. He began to talk lovingly about the world and his vision for it.

"There will be peace everywhere," he said, "and people will have the key to the kingdom within themselves. It's all inside us. The whole of heaven is right here." He pointed to my heart.

Then, suddenly, the *entire* scene changed, and with it, Jesus' appearance. We were in a crowded marketplace in a former time. People were speaking an alien tongue, trying to sell spices and vegetables to the passersby. Jesus' face was brown and worn like those of the people in the market-place. He wore the rags of an Indian *sadhu*. Soon people were all around him, faces bright with love, offering him fruit. He turned to them and spoke in a strange tongue, offering blessings to the hushed crowd.

Then the scene changed again. We were by a quiet stream in a rock garden. Jesus was fat, with almond eyes and a great laugh that rolled out of him in waves that shook the ground. A thin disciple sat quietly near us. A mangy dog appeared and came to the Buddha. The disciple tried to shoo the dog away, but the Buddha stopped him and said, "Watch that dog for his buddha nature."

We seemed to pass through a hundred different scenes, and then we were back in the grove. He was once again the young man I had seen at first.

"Well, who are you?" I asked.

"I live in people's hope," he said.

"Do you have power?"

"People have power. I am a funnel."

"Then how are you different from a politician?"

"They crave power, but how could I? Nobody will follow me but sheep, as you saw. The power *I* have comes from the hope people *find* after a feeling of helplessness. I am just an image, a symbol, around whom much power flows. Find me in the world and we'll bring the kingdom there."

I realized he was saying good-bye. "But wait," I said. "What shall I do?"

"Open your eyes."

I did, and found I was back home again, back in the class-room of the Do-It-Yourself University. It was three in the morning. I was tremendously tired. The whole experience had lasted about six hours.

The next day was Saturday. When I wakened late in the morning, the sun was streaming in the window. I was full of a vast, simple sense of the holiness of life. It was a solemn joy; just to breathe was sweet. I got up and dressed. Each action seemed precious. Walking around the campus I felt as if I were looking at the world with new eyes.

After a while I went to the school's auditorium and sat in the dark, empty space. I watched a friend, the solitary figure on stage, practice a modern dance step. A pink spotlight was the only light in the big room. I was very happy, but I didn't know why.

Even though the figures I had seen and met in this vision appeared as real as my dormmates and my life in the day, I did not think they actually existed. I did not believe that I had been transported to another plane of existence through some cosmic magic. I just called the figure I met "Jesus" out of convenience. Actually, I could have called him "Buddha," "Krishna," "Moses," "Mohammed," or any of the other names of great Christ-like figures throughout history. I was not, therefore, running out to buy a Bible or getting revved up to spread the word on the gospel circuit. I felt intensely happy, but I also felt subdued, reflective.

This vision had been full of dark, rich, medieval Christian pageantry and images. Since these were not a part of my everyday experience or my cultural background, I wondered where they came from. Why were they imbued with such passion and influence in the deepest part of my mind?

My friend had stopped dancing to have a cigarette break. She sat on a metal chair on the side of the stage and the smoke floated slowly under the pink light.

I thought of my childhood. Mine was a particularly unreligious family, but when we had lived in Manhattan I had known many Catholic children. When I was six or seven, we lived on Seventy-second Street and First Avenue. Ours was a high rise on the corner, but down the block were poorer, Irish children who lived in smaller buildings. Since I went to Brearley and they went to parochial school, there was a great deal of confusion when we tried to play school together. I was continually baffled over the family relationships of the large array of fathers, sisters, and mother superiors who staffed our pretend school. To add to the problem, one child would often play several parts, at once being a father and a sister. Generally the sisters were more mean-natured than the fathers, and occasionally a nun would come and replace the sisters. The difference between the two, I later learned, had to do with their various orders of origin which to me, at six years old, seemed as complex and arcane as the orders of angels.

From time to time, a real sister on her way somewhere would come over and talk to our little group. I remember once sitting wide-eyed with the others, as the sister explained the variety of sins you would have to commit to enter each of the spectrum of netherworlds between heaven and hell. At the time it reminded me of a large, overgeared machine that might have been invented by some wild backyard welder. I imagined this machine processing the children, inducing them to enter it in the first place by a mixture of fascination and fear.

Besides this childhood introduction, I had very little background in Christian imagery. I had read *Paradise Lost* and seen the stock Hollywood images of heaven and hell, but beyond that, nothing. None of this, however, seemed strong enough to sear these images into my brain with the intensity with which I had experienced them. Finally, I settled on the same explanation I'd come to for the new color: These were archetypal symbols, images like the heroes and villains in myths and fairy tales, which exist with power and import in the deepest part of a person's mind. Somehow, I had linked my mind to the collective unconscious. Jung believed that these images are inborn. They exist inside all people, having been genetically programmed into the circuits of their brains from the experiences of past generations. This concept offers a human equivalent to the genetic map that tells the plover where to fly.

I feel that people are perhaps born with a predisposition for certain kinds of symbols, like the symbol of the savior, but the actual representations are personal to each individual. This is why Jesus appeared to me as a prep-school boy and to the Indians in the marketplace as a weathered-skinned Indian.

My friend was back dancing again. This time she had been joined by a large black student who often worked with her. Their two bodies seemed curiously right together—his large, dark, and strong, hers so light, soft, and fragile. She was now leaping in the air, and his arms carried her higher than you would think the rules of space and gravity should allow.

Where did the power in religious images come from? Jesus said his power came from the hope born after helplessness. Perhaps through these images the conflicts and aspirations of individual people grow from isolated incidents of hope and worry into large abstractions with meaning and importance for the whole of humanity. In religious images, the forces of good and evil, sorrow and joy, hope and desperation, find a stage large enough to accommodate the epic nature of their conflicts.

In my six-hour encounter with this aspect of my consciousness, I had had a tremendously moving experience. But I still did not know the answer to the little boy's question, "Is there God or Is there not God?" I had met Jesus and the others, but I had never met "Father."

Yet I didn't really mind. My experience with Jesus was intense and warm. He was the archetype of Christ, passing through all ages and fitting into each like a monarch butterfly whose camouflage seems to change with the shifting scene. He had a tremendous love, a tremendous hope for our world's future.

The dancers had now gone, turning off the single light and leaving me alone in the cool, dark theater. I sat there awhile and then went outside into the bright afternoon.

Jesus had said he lived in the humble hope that was born out of helplessness. I certainly had that sort of hope. In my simplest child's heart, I had to admit he lived in me.

CHAPTER

8

SOMETIMES WHEN I SLEEP, MY REST IS SO COMPLETE THAT I absolutely forget everything in my adult life and become absorbed into the trusting, deep sleep of a child. Then when I wake up I am surprised to be big. I expect to see the little body I had fifteen years ago nestled happily between the covers. But I quickly remember everything and realize that I am big because I have grown up. This early morning experience is always a happy one, because it once again reminds me that I have not lost anything by participating in the social and moral intricacies of the adult world. It is literal proof that I am still connected with the child's innate understanding of life's integrity that gave me such peace and security at the beginning of my life.

Fresh from a night of this deep rest, I woke up on the first morning of my 1972 school field trip. It felt so good to breathe and stretch. A few days before, I had turned sixteen. I sat up in my sleeping bag and brushed a little sand off it. We were on the Mexican beach, at the shore of the Gulf of California.

We had three boats that we had built ourselves, and our plan was to sail about seventy miles down the coast from here to Guymas. My friends and fellow aspirants to the seafaring life were all still curled up in their sleeping bags. It must have been about five-thirty. There were a few pale stars still left in the light blue brightening sky. The air was cool and unmoving, as if it too were resting.

I looked down the beach at our boats. All three were exactly alike—wooden, nifty little seventeen-foot craft, designed by an old Maine fisherman. Chip, our faculty member on the trip, had worked with the boat's designer, and they were both wildly enthusiastic about the design. They were convinced it was a bold innovation, improving on the classic dory of the fisherman's home region. The boats had taken us three months to make. While we were working we often had consulted Chip's Down-East friend and received not only hints on boat carpentry, but also assorted maritime lore and plenty of advice on how young people should live.

These were jibless yachts. For sails we had square sheets of waterproof Dacron that worked with a sprit boom, like Chinese junks. I had sewn the sails all by myself on the headmaster's wife's zigzag sewing machine. When they were done, I and Timothy Butters, a fellow boatbuilder, had drawn bright distinctive logos on each of the sails so that we could tell them apart from the shore.

Now, in this early morning, the sails, like Timothy, Chip, and our six other friends, were all rolled up ready to begin our voyage today, though right now none of them showed any sign of going anywhere. So I decided, after one last pleasant stretch in the warmth of my down sleeping bag, to get up and take a walk down the beach.

Just before the sun comes up and at twilight, bodies of water seem to become temporarily still—calmed, so a Hopi told me, by the crack between the two worlds of day and night. I walked by the water's edge and felt happy to have the water move over my feet. Up and down the shore there was a dark line of seaweed that marked the farthest reach of the high tide from the night before. In the half light this reminded me of an artistic construction. For miles and miles, there were three colored bands of different widths whose edges exactly mirrored one another. It was like a canvas an artist might have painted with a roller, except that it was made of the sand, the sea's edge, and the passage of time.

The only movement anywhere was made by small goslings, hatched only a few weeks before, pecking in the seaweed. They were looking for food, small crustaceans whose immature shells would still be soft enough for goslings to eat without trouble. The older birds sat on the water and moved up and down together with the calm waves. They rested, not wanting to move too fast until after the sun came up.

I was now wading up to my knees in the warm water. I felt calm and good. Any heaviness that was left over from the winter months was somehow gone from me, lapped away in the movement of the water. Then, with my blue jeans fully soaked, I ran back up on the beach to sit and shiver on the sand and write a little in a journal I was keeping about the trip. Remembering the next day was Palm Sunday, I wrote: "The ocean washes away every trace of drug or alcohol, all my hate, all the world's hate in me. I feel a presence of god, and it is in the sand and the sea and the wave in continuous motion."

Looking to the east, I had a real sense of the earth's roundness. I felt it moving, turning toward the sun, slowly rolling into morning. Then the sun's first great, red rays appeared on the horizon over the water. Far up the beach I could see the light coming, moving west toward me over the still-shaded sand. Away in the distance I heard a bird shriek and his flock take flight when the sunlight reached the place where the flock had rested on the water. By the time the sun reached where I stood, the air was full of graceful, flying birds. They called out to one another, ringing up high in the sky, making daring dives after fish in the sea.

The sea itself seemed to take on this new, more lively spirit. A breeze came up and bits of water were pulled off the now stronger waves. These airborne drops of water caught the sunlight which had now moved down the spectrum from red to orange on its way to its noontime full brilliance in a whiter shade of yellow.

Happy, feeling like a gosling myself, I skipped back to

camp, where my lazy comrades were still in their sacks. It was obvious to me now that the scenery, not my social life, was going to be the highlight of this trip.

Every day we saw new and wonderful things. One day I remember the sky was particularly blue and the water reflected the color almost exactly. By midday a breeze had come up and was whipping up small, choppy waves. These little waves caught the sun on their brief peaks and made little sparkles all around us. The total effect was like sailing through cool fire. Later that day we sailed through what must have been a pelican belt; every mile or so a new flock appeared in the sky. Though this was spring, the time when the new birds are born, the pelican yearlings still had the salt and pepper plumes of adolescence.

At the end of the afternoon we landed on a salt marsh. Behind the beach was a vast tidal bay. At the evening's high tide the entire area was full of water. Then, slowly, as the moon set, the water receded, revealing the topography of the bottom of the bay. Huge sculpted sandbars had appeared by midnight, when I fell asleep watching the changing scene. By early morning, at the first light of day, these wet sandbars had turned into dry dunes of sand and salt, their moisture drunk by the thirsty air. By ten the moon had gone circling off around the earth and the water was refilling the bay. By one, the sandbars were gone and the bay was once again covered with a flat blanket of bright blue water. Watching this exaggerated effect of the tides, I began to try to visualize the effects of tides on the whole globe.

I imagined the earth and the moon as two round balls rolling around each other without touching. Extending out from each of these is an invisible field of force, gravity, that both holds them together and keeps them apart. As the earth turns, the places on its surface which are closest to the moon are affected most strongly by the pull of the moon. Since water is a loose part of the earth's surface—it has no roots to keep it steady—it is free to respond, rising out to the pull of the moon. Thus the ocean's tides. All bodies of water have tides, even small ponds.

When I started to think about why water responded to the tides I tried to think of other loose parts of the earth that might have tides too. I thought: I am loose, free to roam on the earth, and I'm almost all water; maybe I have tides, too. The air most likely has tides as it stretches itself out into space to meet the moon. Maybe even the ground has slight tides. Thinking of all this, I was glad the earth was strong enough to hold us all—the air, the water, the ground, and me—close to it. I lay down and put my cheek on the sand.

When I returned to school, the term was over for all practical purposes. I still had a few classes to attend, but my immediate future was certain: I would graduate from high school in one month. Knowing this, I felt it was only right that I should take up all the cocky leisure-time activities with which seniors are inclined to fill their Junes. I rehearsed for graduation, gave advice and counsel in liberal doses to the students in the lower classes, and discussed authoritatively the relative worths of the many institutions of higher learning my classmates had chosen. And then, before I knew it, school was over. I had graduated and was enjoying a huge graduation night bout of drinking and celebrating with all of my friends. Very quickly the next morning came; so, with a bit of a hangover, I was soon on a jet back to the East Coast, home to East Hampton.

My desire to see the country was not dampened by my unfortunate experience of the summer before. Of course this year there would be no hitchhiking for me, but I still wanted to travel. Like the little mouse in E. B. White's *Stuart Little*, I always feel best when I am traveling north. On my first peregrination into the great green-blue northern spaces of the country, I took my bicycle and rode two hundred miles in one day to Connecticut, which is the first step directly north of Long Island. Then, in another few weeks, on a Greyhound bus, I made it all the way to Boston. And then from Boston it wasn't far to Maine.

One of my pals from school, Wendy Turner, lived on a little island right over the Maine border, a few miles Down East from Portsmouth, New Hampshire. The Atlantic made up the hinterlands of the Turner estate; the north woods was their front yard. After visiting Wendy and her family for a few days—kayaking up and down the rocky coastal shores, running through the woods with the Turners' dogs and visiting boatyards where Mr. Turner worked as a ship inspector—I felt thoroughly adopted into the Turner clan of all-American children. I spent many hours talking with Mrs. Turner that were as meaningful and sweet as talking to my dearest friends. Slowly, as my intended short stay stretched into a week and then ten days, I realized I was falling in love with Maine.

If I could get into school here, I thought, it would give me a splendid excuse to live in a part of the country I was just now discovering. When the admissions office of the University of Maine in Portland said I could come as a special student for the fall and then matriculate in the winter term, I was delighted. I had an endless fascination with how different people lived. For this reason I wanted to live in many areas of the country, staying long enough to get a feeling for the deep and subtle qualities of the region.

My mother, on the other hand, was less than thrilled with my idea to move to Maine. She was about to have me home again for the first time in several years, and here I was, wanting to traipse off for parts unknown. Finally, somewhat reluctantly, she agreed. "Fine," she said, exasperated. "Do whatever you want. But you'll have to support yourself while you are there."

That didn't seem like such a bad deal. In fact, "pay for it yourself" seems like the standard formula for any kind of freedom. Reluctantly I left the Turners' and continued north to Portland. I arranged to stay with David, my old boyfriend from camp, because, as it happened, his family had a house on a little island right off Portland. It was not hard for me to meet my modest expenses with some money I had saved from my yippie business in 1969.

Portland is a wonderful town. When I got off the bus and walked with my bags outside the Greyhound station, I took a deep breath of the salty air. I closed my eyes and thought I was in heaven. Walking over to the wharfs to get the ferryboat to David's island, I saw that all the buildings in the wharf area are brick, and date from the late 1800s. Their construction reflected a loving care and precision not usually found in latter-day work.

Looking at the great brick-arched windows and simple lines, I started to wonder if objects carry around with them their own historical references, independent of the present. This idea first occurred to me when I was walking in the Washington rail station and the stairs suddenly revealed a chorus of footsteps of all the people who had ever passed over them. Then the idea became firmly planted when I had a similar experience with a visual impression.

I was walking down the street in New York when I saw a completely restored Model A Ford drive by. As it passed me, the entire scene changed in front of my eyes. Everything turned into sepia tones and appeared as it did in 1903 when the Model A was new. It was as if this car was dragging its history behind it wherever it went. When the car reached the light, it paused and then turned the corner. Once it was fully out of sight, everything regained its familiar and ordinary appearance.

Walking around the wharf area in Portland, I was struck by a similar transformational quality in the buildings there. Although that first day I did not actually *see* any changes in their physical appearance, gradually, over the year that I lived in Portland, I began to feel that somehow they were imbued with a frontier spirit that was left over, lurking from the time of their construction. This spirit was manifested in the enterprises and activities that took place in the renovated living and business areas around the wharfs.

School started in September, and it was then that I moved from the island to my new apartment on the mainland. Very quickly I realized that going to school by itself would never be enough to satisfy me. Even though I was going to school full time, I just didn't find it very challenging. It was not only the classes themselves which didn't capture my interest, it was also the other students. Most of the other people near to my age—sixteen—were a rather unsophisticated lot. As far as I could tell they were having their first glasses of wine and unchaperoned dates.

These troubles didn't sour me on educational institutions in general, they just gave me the impression that maybe the University of Maine was not the school for me. I wrote a letter to another college I had been considering before— Bryn Mawr, a Seven Sisters school—and asked for an application. This seemed like sufficient action to calm my worries about the future. For better or for worse, I was going to be in Portland for another term or maybe two, so I began to work on what I had really come here for: to enjoy Maine itself.

I rearranged my class schedule in such a way that all my courses were jammed between Tuesday at four o'clock and Thursday noon. This gave me five and a half days every week in which I was a woman without scheduled obligations. In this time I began to explore Portland and meet many of the interesting people who lived there.

Portland is a model "Small is Beautiful" city. It is the perfect size. Although it holds sufficient status for the surrounding areas to allow their own addresses to be subordinated into a Greater Portland phone book, it does not have any metropolitan troubles that seem beyond the power of local Yankee ingenuity to handle. Beyond mere size, the diverse citizenry contributes to Portland's unique social character. There are the city-curious sons and daughters of

Down East farmers, and New York expatriates busily trying to hide their birthplace beneath a ton of woodsmen's clothes from L. L. Bean; there are blue bloods with long pedigrees, and plain hippies whose home is their shoes.

I found a whole community of young people from all parts of the country who had come to Maine attracted by the state's vast, open, almost unwieldy character. Sometimes, in a new place, it is hard to meet people with interests similar to one's own. I did not face this problem in Portland. Once I met a person I liked, it was not long until I met all of his friends. One fellow who particularly impressed me was Tom Bergman, a nineteen-year-old of slight build with hair that fell clean down the middle of his back. Originally Tom was from Westchester County in New York. Enrolled at Goddard College, Tom was in Portland on a work-study program, teaching literature at the "Street School," an experimental high school.

From the first day, Tom and I enjoyed each other's company greatly. We laughed so hard that my stomach actually cramped up from the motion. When I met him, Tom was living in terrible dump with several other people. This place was so bad that huge chunks regularly fell from the ceiling, and paint was likely to fall down in your food if you ate in the dining room.

After a few evenings at Tom's, I knew that if our relationship was to progress much farther, he'd have to move someplace better. We discussed this idea with his roommates and a group of us decided to move in together.

After a week of checking the newspaper ads, we scored on a beautiful, well-kept apartment. It was the exact opposite of Tom's former residence: five neat and clean bedrooms and a large, modern kitchen. We moved in on October first. The front of our new apartment had a rounded window that looked out over the bay. In the morning I could watch the sunrise over the island where I had stayed with David the past summer. The landlord was a charming gay fellow; it was understood that if we didn't give him any problems about his life-style, he'd be the last one to criticize us. "Just pay the rent," he said. It was a splendid setup.

This was the first time I had lived in a communal way. School is something of a communal environment, except the compulsory nature of my stay tended to dull my enthusiasm. From the first moment I moved into my new house I found collective life suited me perfectly. Together my friends and I enjoyed a simple, almost childlike family feeling. One day shortly after we moved in, it snowed and, quick as a wink, we were all out sledding down a nearby hill on pieces of washing-machine boxes. We'd run through the supermarket together and buy an entire cart full of our favorite foods. If we wanted to go out, we often went together, drinking, dancing, and carousing at the local tavern.

People who are used to having *their* house, *their* car, and *their* things exactly where *they* want them have often asked me, didn't I miss my privacy? Generally, I found that I could have all the privacy I wanted, but often what I wanted wasn't privacy but the company of my adopted family.

I enjoyed coming in to have breakfast in the morning and finding George or one of the other people who lived with us, playing the flute or reading some interesting new book I had never read. It gave my life a richness and variation that meant a great deal to me.

Moving into this apartment signaled the beginning of a new and utterly happy, very active part of my life.

We called our commune the Guru Vishnu Co-op. This unorthodox name did not reflect the religious affiliation of any of the members. It was a stroke of pure frivolity that began when we were trying to decide how to list our telephone. When the phone company wouldn't install a phone for the Waterville Street Co-op without an exorbitant deposit and some sort of corporate papers, we thought we should list an individual's name. But whose? Tom Bergman, being one of the commune's leading citizens, suggested "Rose

Kranz," a Jewish name like his own. Some of the gentile members of the commune argued with him and insisted that WASP was undoubtedly the proper ethnic affiliation. The solution turned out to be getting a name from another part of the world entirely. We chose "Guru Vishnu" after a line praising this Hindu God in one of George Harrison's songs.

But New England Bell was not up for any such nonsense. Guru Vishnu was one customer they'd have to *see*, before they installed anything. This was no problem for us. We simply looked around the room and chose Tom to do the impersonation. With his long hair and beard, he was the best candidate. We dressed him up in white pajamas and made our way down to the Bell business office. To enhance Mr. Vishnu's mystery, we decided he should be a silent yogi, like Meher Baba. At the customer service desk I did all the talking while Tom, holding a daisy, smiled beneficently. The young woman at the desk approved the installation and then asked us why a silent character like the guru needed a phone at all. "You'd think letters would be more his medium," she said. Tom turned around and motioned blessings to the Bell employees. We left in haste, continuing down the road to the utility company.

Tom and I were the least transient residents of the Guru Vishnu Co-op, along with Ricky, a jazz musician. Rick was one of the Guru Vishnu Co-op's founding fathers; he had been in on the original move from Tom's tenement. Most of our roommates came and went. All the people who stayed with us at Waterville Street were friends of ours or friends of friends who came to us with the highest references; we never took a stranger. For instance, I'd known George, the flutist, since I'd known Tom. Formerly George had lived in a cabin upstate. When the winter made it too cold to stay there, he came down and joined the Co-op. We expected to lose him in the spring.

Since Ricky was perpetually penniless and George had that

now-you-see-'im, now-you-don't quality, this made Tom and me the money partners in the firm. Every month Tom and I—taking our buck-stops-here responsibility very seriously—would sit down for three hours and argue bitterly. We'd shout and scream and demand to see all receipts. Finally, when all the money matters were settled, we'd have a beer. Once again we became best friends, till the next month. We never brought Ricky in front of this tribunal to demand his rent money. We just assumed he wouldn't have it, so we let him contribute his music instead. At all hours it floated ethereally through the house.

In the middle of October, after I settled into my new apartment, I took a walk down by the wharfs. I came across a small store with a hand-painted sign in the window saying "Good Day Market." Though this was the middle of the day, it was closed, dark inside. On the door was taped another sign. This one was waterstained and faultily typed: "OPEN: Monday 3:45–5:15 Tuesday 11:00–12:00 Wednesday No Thursday No Friday 3:00–7:00 Saturday 6 on." Saturday seemed like the best bet. To me, these sporadic hours expressed the cry of a co-op store in need of love and attention.

I returned the next Saturday and found the store open. My immediate impression on entering was that the Good Day Market seemed more like someone's rustic cabin home than a place of business. There were several people sitting around in overstuffed old-fashioned chairs that had that rescued-from-the-Salvation-Army-look. The way people inside were speaking to one another was quite a surprise. While they appeared to be talking about the heavy issues of management and money, their expressions were sweet, almost amused. I wondered if they had known each other for a long time. Or if perhaps they were from the same family.

Carole, a tall woman with beautiful high cheekbones, was speaking to a man with a huge Peter Kropotkin-style beard. "Listen, this is how you do it," she said, holding a looseleaf book. "Write down what you sell in this book. Add up the money at the end of the day and then add that to what we have in the checking account. Then we'll always know how much money we have."

The bearded man wasn't embarrassed to receive this most elementary financial lesson. He did not lash out with hippie macho, "Who are you to tell me anything?" as I had heard young men do in my political days. Instead he just took the notebook and said quietly, "Good, I really want this store to go well."

I felt I'd found a home. For the next three months I spent almost every day at the Good Day Market, helping in whatever ways I could.

Good Day Market was a nonprofit store. When I first went there it was charging only a 10-percent markup on wholesale prices. This barely covered the rent and heat. Later we took the markup a bit higher, to about 25 percent. It was clear that the store needed two things. The first was the continual need of any retail enterprise: customers.

I started working with Carole and the other people who staffed the Market on some schemes to promote the store. The Portland newspaper was charmed by our dedication, and wrote a full-page article about us. Then we were invited to speak on a local radio station. It was at this point that I realized I had become an unofficial spokeswoman. When the announcer turned up the mikes and the red light went "On the Air," the normally bubbly Market clerks were quiet.

"So what's the purpose of Good Day Market?" the announcer asked. He scanned our silent faces and everyone turned to me.

"Well," I began authoritatively, hoping no one would notice any trace of a shaky-kneed sixteen-year-old in my voice, "the traditional concept of business is to give the customer the highest price that the market will bear. We, at the Good Day Market, however . . ." I continued with a discussion of the nonprofit concept and my ideas on management principles for the New Age. I surprised even my-self that night.

I recognized the second thing that the Good Day Market needed after I had been working there a month. This was steady part-time jobs for the stalwart and committed volun-teers. They needed some employment that allowed them to work together and schedule their time around their Good Day responsibilities. I had been thinking about this problem for several weeks when a friend from Portland politics ap-proached me and asked if I could get a crew together to renovate a floor of a building for his new offices. He opened his wallet and handed me a hundred-dollar bill. "Think about it," he said.

I took the money and realized that construction was the answer to the Good Day employment problem. In a day or so I had drawn up a plan for a company called Portland-Amer-ica Contracting. I needed this elegant name to give me lever-age when I went to open credit accounts at lumber companies and hardware dealers. It was at this time that I began to use my full three names, *Sophia Whitridge Collier,* written in a fanciful script, to sign the Portland-America contracts.

When I went somewhere in person to make an arrange-ment, I always pretended to be a messenger or Ms. Collier's secretary. I didn't want anyone to know I was only sixteen and therefore, by law, not old enough to even make a con-tract.

In doing all of these things, I confess I neglected my schoolwork. In fact, I stopped going to most of my classes altogether. When faced with the lure of closing a three-thousand-dollar deal for Portland-America Contracting in-stead of attending a lecture on seventeenth-century philoso-phy, it was an easy choice. Every day I was busy from the moment I got up to the moment I went to sleep. Soon, I bought a little black executive notebook to list my appoint-ments. I carried it in my blue jeans pocket.

To keep track of the store and the company, I spent most

of my day traveling around meeting with different people: bidding on jobs, setting up health food dinners for one hundred at old age homes, talking to reporters at the local newspaper, convincing the local hip capitalist to lend us his van to pick up our grain in Boston, finding people upstate who might want to go in on a deal with us to buy a whole freight-car load of wheat from Deaf Smith County in Texas. . . .

Once while I was out bidding on a reroofing job with an experienced contractor who helped me out in making estimates, I found out that the building was owned by the top man in the Portland underworld, "Vito." After my contractor-friend and I had looked the job over and made a bid, the owner asked me to come back the next day and sign a contract.

When I arrived the following afternoon Vito was in a jolly mood and asked me to watch some of his "new" films.

"Well, what kind of films?" I asked.

"Blue films, what else?"

I looked at my watch. In an hour I had to be downtown to meet a friend who was going to run against the incumbent Republican old-timer for city commissioner. My friend was a very popular person around town; she was already on the school board and she came from an old Portland family, so I thought she had a chance. "Okay, Vito," I said. "I'll watch a couple of your films, but let me call a friend now in case you give me any trouble."

"You're smart," he said, handing me the phone.

After watching a short film where two players performed in almost every conceivable permutation of position, I looked at my watch again. "So, you make these," I said.

"Yes, I do, and those are nice kids in them. They make a lot of money like this. Construction is no business for a young woman—do you think you'd like to do a few of these for me?"

"You think making funky little dirty movies is a nice business for a young woman? I think you are an asshole. And if this is the reason you asked me up here . . ." I was getting up to leave when he interrupted me.

"Listen, I didn't think you'd want to do them. I heard you on the radio and I think you are a great lady." He reached into his desk drawer and got out a package of organic candy from the Good Day Market.

"You are a creep," I said, "but if you want to do something for me, you can get me a zoning variance permit for Good Day Market."

"No problem." He smiled proudly. "I've got a man on the zoning board. But what do you want it for?"

"Parking. We need some extra space," I said.

He looked at me, amused and incredulous. "Parking? Parking? I do deals with the zoning board that make me thousands of dollars and you, a smart lady like you, want me to get you a zoning permit so that you can sell granola at a 20-percent markup. I can't believe it, but I'm going to do it."

In late December I was sitting in the store when I got a call from Bryn Mawr. The sweet woman on the other end said my application was very promising. She was sure I would be accepted, but could I arrange to visit an alumni and have an interview?

This call was like a snowflake falling out of the blue sky. I wrote down the name of the person and hung up the phone. I had completely forgotten about my application to college. I looked at the name on the paper and decided to put off calling her for awhile.

Shortly afterward, my mother invited me to spend Christmas in New York with her. Before leaving I wrapped up all of my current contracts and let everyone take a vacation. When the last job was complete, I got on a plane and flew to New York. I stayed a few weeks and enjoyed the leisure. In my mother's apartment were the journals I had written when I was at Verde Valley. Reading about the New Color I had experienced in the Arizona desert, I had a sense of yearning. I wondered if somewhere in the hurly-burly of Good Day Market and Portland-America Contracting I'd misplaced my spiritual interests. Even though my capitalist ventures were not strictly conventional, I wondered if something very common had happened to me: in the excitement of action, I'd forgotten reflection, let it slip away unnoticed, lost between the lines in my appointment book.

When I got back to Portland, I found several of the main Portland-America employees had lined up jobs in a sail factory which had recently opened. Their hours were good, so it seemed like there really wasn't much need for me to get back in the business. Phew—I wiped my brow in relief. Although I loved the heavy schedule and the intense involvement with people, I welcomed a break. I needed to renew my concentration on spiritual things. One of the things on my list to think about was whether to go to Bryn Mawr.

The only way I could approach this question was through the Do-It-Yourself University. I needed some advice on the syllabus, so I went down to the local spiritual bookstore and bought some ecumenical selections from the scriptures. I planned to read, meditate, and write down my reflections.

In the meantime, a new person had moved into the Guru Vishu Co-op. This was Tracy, a young lady with a real guru. Since my mind was now mostly on spiritual subjects, she and I grew close. We talked a lot and walked on the beach. Her guru was a young man no older than I. His name was Guru Maharaj Ji and all of his followers were called "premies," which is Hindi slang for "lovers of God."

CHAPTER

9

PREMIES HAD BEEN COMING INTO THE GOOD DAY MARKET FOR several months, trying to get us to stock their magazine, . . . *And It Is Divine.* Each time they came in, we, always ecumenical and easygoing, politely refused, telling them it wasn't our purpose to carry religious, political, or spiritual writing.

"We just want to sell good, cheap food here," I would say, and invite them to have a cup of our special cinnamon grog. Usually they would stay and talk about their nonphilosophy and nonpolitics.

"To change the world," they said, "you have to change the hearts of the people in the world. As long as there is anger and hatred inside people, there will always be war and murder."

This idea had struck a sympathetic chord in me all along. It paralleled my own social philosophy. When I was doing yippie acts, I felt the aim of my antics was to create Zen-type situations in which people's calm acceptance of the status quo would be shattered, and they would be able to see things in a new way. And now, with my growing concentration on my own spiritual nature, I was open to hearing about personal as well as societal benefits of what a spiritual group might offer.

"Knowledge (the name of their brand of meditation) is the only thing which is going to do it for people," they would insist emphatically. Since I had already been practicing meditation, I knew of the profound effects it could have on me. But the only way? That was something out of a pentecostal reader. My ecumenical sensibilities could not accept it.

"Can we leave a magazine with you?"

"Sure," I said, and stashed it in the box with the *Socialist Worker* another enthusiast had left.

In the past few months I had been too busy to consider doing anything other than my work with Portland-America Contracting and the Market. Just looking after these two projects, I was almost too busy to do my own laundry. But now I had time on my hands. I had put aside an indeterminate period to think about my spiritual life, to read about other people's experiences and revelations, and to meditate, so that I would have some revelations of my own.

This time I did not want to follow the solitary Do-It-Yourself approach exclusively. Even though I'd gotten good results from Revelation 101, I felt I was missing out on the social potential of my spiritual experiences. The insights I was gaining through meditation would be most valuable when I was able to translate them into enlightened actions. To help me attain this goal, I wanted to work with other people who shared this interest. I decided that if I could find a spiritual group that I liked, I would join it.

Spiritual organizations were very un-chic in my circle of friends. All of them agreed it was good to embrace higher values—to be loving, open, and forgiving—but the spiritual discipline so many groups followed seemed hopelessly rigid and incompatible with my friends' flowing "live and let live" way of life. My Portland pals sensed an inherent danger in joining a consciousness-raising group. Every group, they reasoned, has some philosophy, no matter how informal. When you join, you take this philosophy for your own. You make a statement about what truth is. Then, when you think you've found the truth, you start to crusade for it. Even the tiniest amount of crusaderness would have ruined my friends' life-style.

I was aware of this danger, but I didn't think we all had to follow the progression in Dylan's lyric, "I started out on burgundy but soon I hit the harder stuff." Just as all marihuana users didn't go on to heroin, I believed I could get the benefits of communal spirituality without falling prey to the perils.

My quiet decision to join a spiritual group was very much like someone's decision to buy season tickets to the opera for the first time. Certainly, without risking any danger of a bad performance, you could buy a stereo system and the finest recordings of the pieces you would hear on this year's opera program, but it certainly wouldn't be the same. There is something about being there live with all the musicians and other opera fans that makes the experience more beautiful than the one you would have alone.

This increased sympathy toward organized spirituality first made me begin to pick up Tracy's copies of the *Divine Times,* a newspaper put out by Divine Light Mission. In general I found the leader of the organization, Guru Maharaj Ji, to be a witty and interesting character. I identified with him. For a sixteen-year-old spiritually minded entrepreneur like me, there was an undeniable charm in a fifteen-year-old guru who drove around in a Rolls-Royce. He seemed like a marvelous yippie. Even though I didn't agree with all of his ideas and concepts, I had to respect him just as I had respected Abbie Hoffman in his days of outrageousness.

After a month or so of casual perusing, I ran across an article that said Rennie Davis had joined the organization. I remembered Rennie from my political days, so I read the article with great interest. In a long interview, Rennie described his spiritual experiences with the "Knowledge," the spiritual path prescribed by Guru Maharaj Ji. He said that for most of his life he had believed that Marx was right in asserting that the situations people face in society are the causes of the ideas they have. Now, after spending a few months with Maharaj Ji in India, he had switched into the

Hegel Camp, and believed that actually the ideas people have are what created the situations.

" 'Religion' comes from the word 'realization,' " he said, "and I now see that religion is far from 'the opiate of the people.' Real religion, like Knowledge, will actually be the People's savior."

He now felt that the work of the peace movement, in which he had labored so long, would not bring any society-wide changes. Instead, he "envisioned a spiritual movement with the aim of raising the collective consciousness of the nation as the first step toward any other meaningful change."

Although this idea was not really new to me, when I read it in Tracy's newspaper it seemed to click. Maybe Divine Light Mission could help me with both my personal spiritual aspirations and my hopes for the world.

Of course I wasn't completely sure. The Divine Light Mission was a mixed bag. Some of the premies who came into the Good Day Market seemed to be nothing more than local "bongos," so "high" that they were tripping over their feet. And then there was that name—"Divine Light Mission." Can you imagine naming anything that? It was awful, a real embarrassment. It sounded like the sort of thing you might see while driving through the Deep South on a small tar road. There would be a little white clapboard church building with an old sign out front: "First Church of the Divine Light Mission." And then about another ten miles later, there would be a "Second Church of the Divine Light Mission," but you'd never see another anywhere.

Putting these prejudices aside, I decided to go to New York and visit the offices of Divine Light Mission there. I wanted to find out more; to meet other people in the DLM and learn what, if anything, their brand of meditation had to offer me.

When I arrived, I was greeted by a pile of shoes and coats at the door of the old church where DLM had its home in the Big Apple. Through a curtain, I heard some people talking. I entered quietly and joined a small circle of people reclining on the floor around a very fat American in an overstuffed chair. Pointing a fat finger at a hippie-looking young man, he said, "Your ego is in your hair."

He paused dramatically after this revelation and then continued, "I asked you if you would cut that hair of yours for this Knowledge, and you hesitate. Obviously, you do not value your spiritual life very much. Hair grows back, but spiritual wisdom is forever. Think about this." He stared intensely at the embarrassed hippie for a long time.

"Okay," he concluded, staring, "are there any questions?"

"Well, what about eating? You are very fat. You must be very attached to food," a young woman suggested. This did not faze the fellow in the chair.

"Hahahahahaha." Laughter rolled out of him. With a wave of the hand, he excused us all. "Come back tomorrow."

After I left the room where the fat man was seated (I later learned he was a local devotee), I wandered around the DLM headquarters and met several other more reasonably sized and sounding premies. I returned the next day to see a "mahatma," the title given to the premies who teach the meditation techniques. Before the mahatma came, many premies got up and testified to their experiences with the "Knowledge." While some of the short talks had the "Now I'm saved, Praise the Lord" sound about them, others were introspective and well said. All of them were almost painfully sincere. In as many ways as people spoke, the message was told: Knowledge is a simple, easy way to improve yourself and the world.

Although I was dubious about a balm with such universal effectiveness, a panacea for all ills, I was struck by the honesty and sincerity of the people who testified. If even a small part of what they claimed was true, as Rennie had said in his interview, "this is joyous news."

As I tried to decide if I should learn the techniques of meditation, one young woman's remark tipped the scales in favor of staying. She said since she had been meditating, she even enjoyed ironing and doing dishes. The Guru Vishnu Co-op needs this, I thought, and filled out the index card that the mahatma was passing around to the people who wanted to give the Knowledge a try.

When the cards were collected, the mahatma read off names and asked about our spiritual goals. The mahatma was an older Indian man, who spoke with a characteristic whining accent. Often in his questions he quoted the scriptures and made large gestures to emphasize points. From about a hundred names, he picked out thirty—including me— and told the rest to keep coming back and listening to more about DLM. Then, with the others gone, he turned down the lights and a conspiratorial tone came into his voice.

"You are about to learn the holiest of all secrets," he said. "All religions are based on the principle that the Kingdom of Heaven is within each person; that each person is part and parcel of God. Every person can know and realize this. It does not matter where someone is from, what the sex may be, or what is the class or creed. Every human being can be intimately connected to this heavenly kingdom, within himself, if he has the key to unlock the door. This Knowledge is the key and you are going to learn it today. Of course, when you have this key, it is up to you to use it. The aim of human life is to realize God, and that takes much effort and work. When I say realize God, I do not mean to know intellectually, 'Sure, God is within me,' but instead, to experience it practically—to feel the love and wisdom of God within oneself, with every breath and action.

"Guru Maharaj Ji has the divine mission of taking this Knowledge to all people. By learning these techniques today, a bond of love and commitment is made between you and Maharaj Ji. By taking this Knowledge you become disciples, and you must follow his counsel to the letter if you want to progress and realize union with the God inside of you in this lifetime."

After this introduction, the mahatma asked for questions. "Why the intense reverence of the guru?" an older woman wanted to know. "I saw people bowing before his picture; surely you can follow this spiritual path without doing this."

"Oh, sister," the mahatma said, "to me Guru Maharaj Ji is my divine father. I love him more than the whole world. He has taken me from the darkness of illusion and moved me into a world of light. To me, he is the Lord himself standing on the earth. I melt in the love he has shown me. I bow to hide my face before him. Of course, in the Bible it is written, 'By his fruits you shall know him.' Take this Knowledge and discover if Guru Maharaj Ji will mean as much to you as he means to me. For a Western person, this is hard to understand. You are so proud. But look at it this way. If you have a dollar bill in your pocket and it falls out, you will bow and bend to pick it up. Even for a penny you will stoop. So for this supreme Knowledge of God, should you not do as much as you would for a penny?"

All of this heavy religious talk was surprisingly easy for me to translate into my secular idiom. I heard the mahatma saying: "Take this meditation and practice it. If you like it, take the guru too. Go along with him as long as he helps you. And if there comes a point where he no longer helps you, just leave."

I thought it all sounded very fair.

The meditation techniques were very simple and effective. When I tried them out with the group, I felt wonderful calm and joy. There were four techniques concerned with bringing the practitioner in contact with certain internal experiences of light, sound, taste, and "vibration." Three of these techniques were for formal, or sitting meditation, and the fourth was for anytime. This last one was particularly interesting, because you could do it while you were walking around or riding on the bus or doing anything else. Because this fourth technique is such a practical and sensible solution to everyday stress and strain, I am going to tell you how to do it here.

Dr. Herbert Benson of the Harvard Medical School wrote a book called *The Relaxation Response,* where he explains that in every person there is a built-in ability to relax. It is the nervous system's answer to the "fight or flight" response. In order to bring about the "relaxation response," Dr. Benson said, several things are necessary. One of these is an object on which to concentrate your attention, like a word or phrase. This is called a mantra. Another thing is a proper setting, a quiet place in which to repeat the mantra to yourself.

This is basically the TM approach to meditation. Guru Maharaj Ji, on the other hand, had an even simpler and more functional way to bring on the relaxation response.

Our breath is a naturally built-in mantra, always flowing within our chests. When you gently turn your awareness toward the movement of your breath, its continuous rhythm will have a soothing effect on you. Beyond being merely soothing, this is also exhilarating. At the top and bottom of the breath, there is a little experience of energy surging within your body. As you concentrate on this little spark, it gradually becomes more pronounced and invigorating. Because you are concentrating on your own breathing, something which is going on within you at all times anyway, this meditation does not detract from your experience of other activities. You can still follow the intrigues of TV crime dramas while you meditate; the only difference is that you will be in touch with yourself in the most basic and beautiful way while you are staring at the tube.

After the mahatma had taught us all four techniques, he said that the reason for our positive experience was the connection of grace that was established between us, the disciples, and Maharaj Ji, the Guru, in this mystical initiation. We should not teach the meditation to anyone else, he cautioned. The people we taught would be spiritual bastards, initiates without gurus. And furthermore, he added, if we taught the meditation to anyone else, we would suffer too, if not in this life, in the hereafter. Undoubtedly we would be reincarnated as snakes, he said.

To me this seemed like typical Hindu mumbo-jumbo. I felt that there was good reason to safeguard the first three techniques of meditation. They were more advanced and should be learned in a certain setting, like a Knowledge session, where everything could be properly explained and all questions answered. But I thought Indian threats were not a good way to protect them. Hellfire and brimstone, from whatever culture, just isn't that scary.

The Divine Light Mission plan for God-realization did not consist of meditation alone. It had suggestions on how to approach every aspect of daily life. The first and most basic part of the prescription was meditation in doses of an hour in the morning, an hour at night. Then came service. Service was roughly equivalent to the Buddhist idea of "right livelihood." Any activity you did should be spiritually elevating. You should not engage in any employment you found immoral or that hampered your spiritual growth. Ideally, everything you did should be selfless. After service came *satsang*. This is a Hindi word that means "the company of truth," and it generally refers to conversation about the spiritual realization and experiences of the conversants. *Satsang* also is used to refer to meetings of groups of premies for the purpose of talking over spiritual subjects on a more formal basis.

All of this comprised a way of looking at life, rather than any particular doctrine. If people practiced meditation, service, and *satsang*, in whatever form these might take in their life-style, they certainly would have a beautifully focused spiritual life. And this was exactly the kind of thing I was looking for.

As it happened, there were several premies at this initiation whom I knew from the Good Day Market, and I was able to catch a ride north with them. All the way back to Portland, I meditated in the car. At about three in the morning, I arrived on my steps at Waterville Street in a state of ecstasy. Immediately I went upstairs and woke up Tracy, to tell her I had received Knowledge. She was so happy for me that she jumped out of bed and kissed me.

CHAPTER
10

AFTER MY INITIATION INTO KNOWLEDGE I FOUND MYSELF IN an uncompromised state of bliss that lasted almost eight weeks without pause for a tear or sad thought. Day after day I woke up to discover I was still overjoyed. The smallest things—walking to the Good Day Market with the cold on my face; drinking a cup of hot tea, smelling the steam; or seeing a tiny place where the ice on the street was melting, making beautiful colors as the light came through it—all were rich, precious experiences for me.

The Knowledge was turning out to be everything that it was chalked up to be, and more. For the first time I understood Lao-tzu's remark, "Those who say don't know, and those who know don't say." There was no way for me to "say" the tremendous feeling of steady-state ecstasy I knew in my heart. It was simply past the reach of words or even understanding.

Yet, unfathomable as it seemed, my transformed consciousness produced surprisingly concrete effects in me and in other living things I encountered.

One day I was walking along in the freezing March air to visit an old friend. The total trip was about two miles, which when made on foot should have been distance enough to freeze the most hearty north-country bones. However, as I walked I found I was getting warmer and warmer. The joy I felt in my chest was swelling up to such an extent that it was

118

actually heating my body. First I unzipped my coat; by another quarter-mile I had to remove it altogether because I was so warm.

Soon after, as I walked on, I reached a large plumbing-supply yard. I was attracted to the shapes of the huge conduits, which looked interesting in the snow. Trooping across the yard seemd like a fine and fun shortcut. When I was about halfway across the lot, a huge dog came running out of nowhere, barking and growling. When he reached me, he jumped up and put his feet on my chest. His huge head and open mouth were only about three inches from my face. Somehow I was not scared at all. Not once did I feel any adrenalin rise in my blood. In fact, it didn't even occur to me that the dog meant me any harm. All I felt from him was the weight of his paws and the warmth of his breath on my face.

The dog looked confused by this behavior. With his paws still on my chest, he turned his head first one way and then the other, as dogs do when they are puzzled. Then he jumped down and started wagging his tail and licking my hand.

I patted the dog on the head and walked on. Only the next day did I realize that I had encountered a *guard* dog. In the fullness of my own joy, I had assumed that the dog was running over to greet me and had jumped on me in his enthusiasm.

To some people this story may sound hopelessly spaced out. "The girl joins the guru and then she can't even tell when a dog is attacking her," they might say. But when you are inside such an experience it is quite different. It is powerful proof that in a very practical way you *can* change the world by changing your consciousness. When I met the dog I was feeling an indivisible connection with my own loving nature, and this feeling, like the alchemist's stone, transformed everything I came into contact with.

On another occasion, a month or so later, I was sitting in the woods meditating. My eyes were closed, and in front of them I saw only a luminous haze of slowly swirling golden light. In this tremendous state of peace, I felt like one of the old red rocks back at Verde Valley. Then something touched me. Slowly, I opened my eyes. A chickadee was sitting on my shoulder with its tiny, delicate legs holding the hem of my sleeve ever so lightly. I looked deep into its eyes and it began to sing.

People, on the other hand, did not always react so positively. The manager of my bank told me to stay away from gurus. "They are all cheats. It's no good for a girl like you."

When I called up Vito, my friend from the Portland underworld, he hung up on me in mid-conversation. When I called him back, believing I had been disconnected, he wouldn't answer the phone. Finally, after several weeks, he called me back and apologized.

"Listen, kid," he said. "You don't need to do this. People join these groups because they are failures. They're burnt out on drugs and are just looking for the next thing to help them escape it all, but you're a nice kid. You're a real winner."

After half an hour he gave up trying to convince me.

"Okay, okay," he said. "I never did understand you. So, good luck."

At home, my friends were interested, but somewhat skeptical about my new guru and my happy way of looking at life. "You sure you're not on STP?" one housemate asked me several times, referring to the hallucinogenic drug that provides a thirty-six- to forty-hour trip. I spent hours sitting around the kitchen table, answering questions with Tracy. In a few days Ricky, the Guru Vishnu Co-op's only musician, wanted to learn the meditation. And several weeks later, two more received the Knowledge. Eventually five people from the market and three from the co-op joined DLM.

During this time my circle of friends grew to include many of the local premies. From them I learned the history of Guru Maharaj Ji's mission from its beginnings in India.

Although it makes little difference to me, many people believe that the reputation of a spiritual group is based on the group's ability to trace the lineage of its leader back to some great soul who is commonly recognized for his miracles and saintly demeanor. The Pope, for instance, gains his authority from his fraternity with all the other Popes, all the way back to Peter and, via Peter, Jesus. If you have ever encountered a saffron-robed Hare Krishna on the street and lingered long enough to listen, you probably know that Indian spiritual groups put an even greater emphasis on the value of a divine lineage than Catholics do.

So, as you may imagine, to trace the history of Divine Light Mission you have to go back several generations. Guru Maharaj Ji's father was a guru before Guru Maharaj Ji was even born. His full spiritual name was Yogiraj Param Sant Satgurudev Shri Hans Ji Maharaj, but let's just call him "Hans."

In the classical tradition of an eastern religious story, Hans was born into a wealthy family. He grew discontent at an early age and left home to go in search of truth. After much traveling and a short stint in a political group, he found a guru who impressed him with a display of power and wisdom. This guru descended from the line of Ramakrishna, a famous Indian saint of the 1800s. Hans spent several years in the service of this guru and became a favored disciple. When the guru died he passed on his spiritual mission to Hans on the grounds that the young man was his true devotee, pure in heart and fully God-realized. Naturally, some of the other close disciples of the late guru were a bit upset about this. They had a favorite candidate of their own for the new guru. So they were determined to stir up trouble. In a graceful move, Hans abandoned them to their infighting and set out on foot to spread the "Knowledge of God" all over India. In many years of traveling, spending the night in rail stations and in fields, Hans attracted a large following, numbering an estimated one million.

Some years later Maharaj Ji's father settled down, married, and had four sons, the youngest of whom was Guru Maharaj Ji. When Hans died in 1966, he assigned the authority of his mission to his son, Maharaj Ji, who was just eight years old at the time. This choice of successor can be viewed in several ways. Maybe Guru Maharaj Ji really was the most pure devotee of Hans and therefore the only one truly fit to carry on his work. Or perhaps Hans wanted to keep "the money" in the family by electing the son he felt could best carry on the family business. Or maybe he was trying to avoid the turmoil which marked his own transition into power after his guru died.

Whatever the reasons, Hans made sure that his son was well prepared for his new role. Two years before, when Maharaj Ji was six, his father had taught him how to meditate, and constantly emphasized its importance. He taught Maharaj Ji English and gave him the opportunity to address the people who came each day to listen to spiritual discourses. Among Hans's followers, little Sant Ji, as he was called then, was a real inspiration and favorite.

In modern America the only examples of small children with religious missions are found on the gospel circuit. It is easy to assume that Maharaj Ji is just another Marjoe, bullied into preaching by his parents. But in India, young children with spiritual wisdom to share are an intrinsic part of the religious heritage. In fact, Krishna, the main Hindu God-incarnate figure, was first noticed for his divine escapades when he was but a wee lad. Popular folk legends in the East are full of tales of young children who have left all to follow God. One entire festival is celebrated every year in honor of Pralad, a nine-year-old whose love of God and guru was sufficient for him to endure great danger and suffering.

With so many role models around, it doesn't seem unlikely that a little Indian boy would want to grow up to be a saint, in the same way American boys wish to be President.

By his own accounts, Maharaj Ji "wanted to be a premie" and "understood the supreme importance of meditation by my own experience." He didn't want to be a guru himself. To me this sounds like the same thing I heard among the wealthy heirs at Verde Valley. They had been in the back rooms of the upper class and now they had graduated. Maharaj Ji's father was a guru, revered by a million people, yet Maharaj Ji saw more freedom in meditating and being "a mischievous little boy."

But, since Hans had died naming him the new Guru Maharaj Ji, he no longer had any choice about it. He recalls feeling a tremendous power coming into him at Hans's funeral. He was seized with a conviction to continue his father's work. This new role put the little Maharaj Ji in a difficult position. Many Indians believe that their guru is like God. Out of the guru's mouth comes the divine will. As the Mahatma said in my Knowledge session, "To me, Guru Maharaj Ji is my divine father . . . he is the Lord himself standing on the earth."

So, in 1966 Maharaj Ji accepted the post, and with it the ambiguity of his own opinion of himself as "a mischievous little boy," contrasted with the position some of the premies put him in: "The Lord of All." In the winter he went to school and in the summer he traveled on speaking tours throughout India, attracting new followers.

By 1969 several Western young people traveling in India had become his disciples. Gradually they convinced Maharaj Ji to come to the West. In 1971, when Maharaj Ji was thirteen, he went to England on his summer vacation. One of my friends met Maharaj Ji when he first arrived there. At that time, this particular friend was a completely outrageous hippie. He wore his very long dark hair puffed out like a dark halo extending half a foot from either side of his white face. He remembers spending an entire day talking with Maharaj Ji about the drug, LSD.

"He loved the idea of it," my friend said, "but he insisted

Knowledge was better. I couldn't convince him to try LSD. And in the end he convinced me to try Knowledge."

If they had gotten Maharaj Ji to come as far as England, some American premies thought they could now get him to come all the way West. "To America, man."

Maharaj Ji's arrival stateside created quite a sensation in the youth culture. I remember hearing about it, even tucked away in Baltimore. Thousands of people were attracted to Maharaj Ji's lectures. With what I thought was a real genius for cultural adaptation, his speeches were filled with frequent references from the life of a young American. Bubble gum, comic books, race cars, rock and roll—all became neat objects for commercial-age parables about self-realization and the nature of the universe.

By the time I received Knowledge in February of 1973 an estimated 35,000 people had learned the meditation and were happily watching their breaths with their new guru.

So what did I think of all this? I knew I was literally having the experience of my life every day, but that was about all I knew. Upon joining DLM I did not accept all DLM ideas as my own. One of the ideas I couldn't go along with was that Maharaj Ji was the Perfect Master, the current incarnation of a divine lineage which included Krishna, Buddha, Mohammed, Moses, Jesus, Ramakrishna, as well as other luminaries.

The reason I couldn't go along with this idea was not because I thought it ridiculous that a fifteen-year-old fat kid from India was the Lord. People from every religion have equally foolish ideas at the very heart of their faiths. Some Hindus believe that Krishna is a four-armed fellow who even to this day dances in the deep forests of northern India. Some Christians think it is possible to rise from the dead, as they claim Christ did. Or maybe, they think the world will end in an angel-wrought torrent of fire, blood, plagues, and pain, as it says in Revelations.

In considering the worth of the DLM belief, I felt it was

actually *more* sensible than most religious beliefs. People believe the sort of thing I mention above solely as the result of hearsay. They hear it in church or they read it in the scriptures. They don't have any firsthand experience of these things at all. No Jew I have met believes that leading an exemplary Jewish life will make the oil in his heater burn even one extra day, though every Hanukah he lights the menorah to commemorate the time in the first century when the Maccabees beat the Syrians and the temple lights burned eight days on one day's supply of oil. In the same season that Jews are celebrating this miracle, Christians are celebrating virgin birth. Yet if the daughter of any one of those Christians came home and dared to suggest that her pregnancy was one inspired without sex, her sanity would be doubted. "But these are miracles, one-time-only events," some might defend their faith. All I can say is, there is no way to know if these things even happened at all, let alone how they happened.

Premies who believe that Guru Maharaj Ji is the Lord have at least *some* actual basis for their belief. Through the Knowledge, most premies were experiencing an unusually great degree of happiness and peace of mind. Given my own experiences in Knowledge, if I were a religious person, I might easily have thought Guru Maharaj Ji was the Lord. After all, through the Knowledge he had taught me to do something I had wanted to do all my life and had never been able to. He taught me to consciously unlock the kingdom of energy, power, and love inside myself, to get back inside of the East Hampton wave on a permanent basis. Now from all signs, that deepest want in me was satisfied. At any time I wanted to, I could meditate and be right there. For a religious person this could easily seem like adequate proof for identifying a divinity.

As a religious concept, "the Perfect Master" idea has some merits beyond the subjective analysis of people's firsthand testimony. I find it much more hopeful to think that if God existed he would come to earth to ensure the salvation of the "righteous" members of *every* generation, rather than to appear once and leave a legacy in the form of scriptures on which subsequent generations must depend for their help. If every religion is based on the life and mission of a particular Perfect Master, then this promotes unity among different faiths. It makes it impossible for a Christian to call the Hindus "heathens," because Krishna—the "Lord" who lived 5,000 years ago in the Indian forests—was an earlier form of the "Lord" who appeared 3,000 years later as Christ.

Despite all of these good points I could not buy into the idea that Maharaj Ji was God. For one thing, I did not believe in any all-knowing, all-powerful God. In my mind, God never came to earth in *any* incarnation. As for the lives of Krishna, Buddha, and all the rest, I did not have any basis on which to determine if any of them lived at all, particularly as described by their followers, or if they were just a strong dream that captured the minds of generation after generation.

Beyond my religious doubts, I had some doubts about Maharaj Ji himself. From listening to the stories of his activities, I believed I knew him a little better than to think he was divine. Mostly, to me, Maharaj Ji was a charming teenage prankster, a future friend.

To add to these hesitations, my mother pointed out something else to me. With the dry humor I love in her, she said, "Having such *vast* experience of the universe, you really are in a position to nominate someone as 'Lord.'"

Hell, I haven't even been to Europe.

In the month after I had received Knowledge, several other people from my household went to learn the meditation with similar happy effects. Once we were all together trying to do meditation, *satsang*, and service, it was easy for us to see how our previous way of living was glaringly inconsistent with our new hopes. It didn't seem right to be discussing cosmic consciousness in our traditional talking place, the kitchen, when dishes were piled in the sink from the night before. Some of our bills were a month overdue, just from carelessness. Someone in the co-op had written away to a lot of book clubs to get their books and never paid a cent for them. Looking around, one thing seemed obvious. It was time to clean up our act, as individuals and as a household. In a blissful but bumbling way, we reasoned, "If Knowledge is a path to God, our aim is to become saints."

(Gradually, as I spent more time considering the incorporeal side of life, I adopted the word "God" to describe a certain feeling I had for the unity of creation. After this, the other words that surround the concept of God—"grace," "saint," "purity . . ."—began to slip into my vocabulary. These words aren't exactly accurate for me to use because I have little feeling for God as a superior power or for saintliness as a moral concept, and those are the traditional ways in which these words are employed. Nonetheless, I didn't feel compromised by using them. I adopted them with the same mix of convenience and confoundment that prompted a group of subatomic physicists who were studying "Quarks," infinitesimal particles, to name the Quarks' characteristics "Charm," "Strangeness," "Flavor," and "Color." As one of the researchers remarked: "It is all a great mystery to us. We know they exist. And we know they do things. And perhaps they are even holding this entire universe together, but how they are doing it, and why, well, I have to shrug my shoulders. I don't know."

With this highest goal of saintliness firmly in our sights, though admittedly quite a spell down the road from our actual position, we started trying to purify our lives from any taint of worldliness. As had been promised on the day I joined Divine Light Mission, I actually did develop a penchant for ironing and washing dishes. As a group, the Guru Vishnu Co-op settled all of its bills. We sent the books back to the book clubs and in general tried to make friends with all our past adversaries. We started to keep regular hours, cooking our meals together with "love and consciousness" and swallowing each well-chewed mouthful in monastic silence.

All this would have been great, except that there were still people living at the Guru Vishnu Co-op who liked it just fine the way it was before their friends "got religion." Naturally, all of this compulsive activity came as a surprise to these heathen members of the household. At first Sophia-Tom-Ricky-and-Tracy's "guru trip" was viewed with sympathy and amusement. But after a short time, our friends had enough of our odd behavior. I think the last straw came when Tracy asked the landlord to take off his shoes before he came into the house.

There is no one quite so impatient as someone who has just learned something. The newly mature, my mother says, are the most intolerant of all people. They expect everyone to know what they know and they want them to know it now.

After another week or so we met some people who had been meditating longer than we had and they suggested we cool out our trip. While silent meals and fanatic dishwashing may seem like the peak in Zen awareness to you, the older premies explained, to others they are nothing more than a petty annoyance, plain foolishness that will serve to alienate people from any spiritual wisdom you might have.

The widening differences between Guru Vishnu Co-op residents made it clear that the time had come for the household to split up. The reasonable thing to do seemed for the premies among us to find another place to live where we could pursue our specialized goals without bothering our friends.

Several other premies wanted to move in with us too, so we decided that in order to avoid the same problems we had at the Co-op, we should sit down and discuss exactly how each one of us wanted to live. In the end we decided to organize our new household like an *ashram*. Many groups, including DLM, have ashrams—spiritual residences organized in a monastic tradition. DLM was maintaining forty-eight ashrams in the United States at this time. We were not an official *ashram,* but each of us decided to take informal vows of poverty, chastity, and obedience according to the following definitions of these vows.

"Poverty" meant that the group would work as one person financially. Each person would give his paycheck into the common pot and then be cared for completely by the group. Everything that we used we agreed to own communally, respecting "habitual" use and common sense.

Another side of our financial life that we all agreed on was that each person in the house should have some kind of gainful employment, except for one person who would operate as a houseparent and take care of the others. Not in the mood to seek any "gainful employment," I volunteered for this job and was accepted on the scant credentials of my ability to make oatmeal and operate a washing machine.

"Chastity" meant no sex—at least not in the house, or with the other residents.

And "obedience" meant that once you moved in, until the day you moved out, you would cooperate with and work toward the goals of the group, in other words, poverty and chastity, *satsang,* service, and meditation. To help us fit all this in we adopted a simple schedule.

Since time immemorial, people have argued over the virtues of monastic life. But regardless of whether it is the best way to live, you can see that it is very practical. We all agreed that it would certainly simplify our personal lives and household hassles.

At this time Tracy decided to move into the real ashram in Boston. She always was a Massachusetts girl at heart. Since Tracy was, coincidentally, one of my only female premie friends, I was left alone to begin my first days of monastic life with a group of charming young men.

Right from the start we had a real family feeling. As the

housemother I fixed meals. On Sundays I made muffins and brought them out to the table still steaming. I felt like a mother on a farm serving her brood of grown-up sons. On weekends, we all piled into the car and drove off to visit some friends who lived on the beach. Together we meditated late into the night, relishing the stillness of the hours after midnight. In the morning we played on the beach, running, laughing, and chasing each other, high as kites from our meditation the night before.

When we had started living together in the beginning of March, we had felt as though we were beginning an experiment. Now, after three months of communal monastic life, we thought we might do something which would make our life together more permanent. Our apartment was really a bit too small for all of us to spread out comfortably, so we decided to buy a house. "Poss," the wealthiest member of our household, said he would finance the purchase and, if anything went wrong, the house would be his and he could just sell it. With real estate values going up, who knows, he'd probably even make a profit.

After several weeks of checking the real estate listings, we found a beautiful house that was exactly what we were looking for. It was built at the turn of the century, but was extremely well cared for. In almost every room there was intricate oak woodwork and built-in leaded glass cabinets. The kitchen had counters of marble and slate.

There were plenty of rooms for all six current residents, and a few extra for new additions to our spiritual family. At the top of the house there was even a special room that we thought could be for Guru Maharaj Ji if he ever came up North.

Thinking about buying a house made me realize how much I cared for the people I lived with. Sometimes I laughed to myself, thinking, I'm only seventeen and already I'm in love with six people. In my service as housemother I tried to look after each one of them and take care of his personal needs. This love was not a one-way street. It seemed whatever I gave out of my heart came back to me multiplied. In particular I remember the day my two-month period of joy broke. Early in the morning I had had a haunting dream. I was in New York riding on a public bus. Somehow I had gotten into a conversation with the man sitting next to me. After some chatting, he asked me what I did in Maine. I told him about Knowledge. When he realized this meant Eastern spirituality, he made fun of meditation and the people who practiced it, in the same manner I had seen in popular magazines.

"I don't think you understand," I insisted. "Did you ever have a feeling of the vast awesome mystery that surrounds life? Did you ever want to expand your awareness so that you might understand that mystery?"

My question made him mad.

"Look." He took out his wallet from his back pocket. Showing me a wad of C-notes, he said, "This is all the awareness I need."

I looked deep into his eyes. They were a rich chestnut brown. As I watched, their appearance changed. The man's eyes seemed like windows into another world. Through them I could see the dark blue color of a starless night sky.

When the man blinked, his chestnut-colored eyes reappeared. In this brief look I felt I had seen the infinite part of him. I had seen his "Buddha nature," the Kingdom of Heaven within him. That this man would have the potential for enlightenment inside him and not even be aware of it was a pathetic tragedy that I felt was common to many people in the world.

I woke up crying. This was the first morning that I was not in the elated state that had become my normal consciousness for the past few months. When I went to cook breakfast I was still sad. I served food and went to cry alone in the kitchen. Finally, at mid-morning, Poss came in and asked what was wrong. The sincerity of his love and concern struck me right away. But often when I am sad and crying, someone acting sweet toward me only makes me cry all the harder.

Poss stayed and I told him about the dream.

He said, "Soph, I believe the New Age is coming. Why do you think we are called Divine Light *Mission*? It's because we have a mission. And that's to help people to discover what we have found, to know within themselves the highest love."

In my sad mood, I just didn't see how such a thing could work. It would take magic to fix up this world and bring a new age.

"Let's take a drive in the country," Poss suggested. But even as I watched the early signs of spring pass by the car window, I still felt sad.

Poss was now at his wit's end. "Okay," he said. "There is one thing I know how to do that will cheer up a girl. It is something my father taught me."

I was interested to hear what this might be, remembering Poss's upper-class Maine background. He turned from the country road and drove to a nearby town. Pulling over at a fancy shop, he said, "Why don't you buy some new clothes on me. Anything you want." He handed me his charge card.

To some people this may reek of old-fashioned male chauvinism, but to me it was one of the sweetest things anyone had done for me in quite a while. It made me feel much better. With my packages in hand at the end of the day, I remembered my dream. If that man only knew what a little money *and* a little meditation can do for your life, I thought, smiling.

This dream proved sobering. More than before, I was struck with a sense of purpose in practicing Knowledge to increase my own awareness and in telling other people about it so that they might experience the same benefits as I.

One day Poss and I were sitting around the dining table talking about where the money was going to come from to buy the house. I was helping him sort out his assets, considering which ones he should liquidate.

"I have some money coming when I am eighteen," I offered, to match his investment, if not in dollar amounts, with my commitment.

"Eighteen, that's two years!" Poss laughed.

"No, no," I corrected. "Remember, I had my birthday. I'm seventeen now."

In our household, people frequently teased me good-naturedly about my youth. Poss knew very well I was seventeen because he lit the candles on my birthday cake.

In the midst of this good-humored talk, the phone rang. It was the Boston DLM office calling us. Poss got on one extension and I took the other.

"So what's up in the woods?" a voice asked us.

We told about the new house we had found and our plans to buy it. Expecting them to be glad, we were shocked by the response.

"That's simply the worst idea we've heard yet," the voice said. "You heard about the festival we're having this fall in the Astrodome?"

"Sure, we read about it in the *Divine Times*."

"Well, who do you think is gonna pay for it? If you've got money like that you should send it to Denver, to National Headquarters. If we all work together *as a group* we can spread Knowledge. We can bring peace. But when premies are all looking out for their own little trips, in their own little towns, it's not going to work at all.

"Bay Bhagwan Ji, Guru Maharaj Ji's brother, is in charge of the festival. He's going to be in Boston next weekend to speak about it. You guys better come. This festival is our biggest outreach effort. You must have read what the national treasurer said in the *Divine Times*: 'Divine Light Mission is an emerging nation.' Well, this festival in the Astrodome is our birthday party where the whole world is invited to hear our message.

"Look, don't buy the house. Send the money to Denver and come to Boston to hear Bal Bhagwan Ji speak. You can fill out skills forms there. Who knows, they might need you to do service at Houston putting the festival together. Remember, this is a national movement." The voice hung up abruptly.

Poss and I looked at each other in amazement. We slowly replaced the receivers. Poss shrugged his shoulders with a smile on his face. We both felt excited but a little confused.

"National movement?" Poss said. "Goodness, we don't want to miss that."

CHAPTER

11

ONE DAY LATE IN APRIL I TOOK A WALK IN THE SPRINGTIME rain. I was alone on the streets except for the brief company of a man who hurried past me huddled under an umbrella. It was raining hard, and the water made the sidewalks shine. The water was warm; I enjoyed feeling the rain as it soaked my sneakers and head. Everywhere under the earth I could feel the spring growing, gathering momentum, ready to burst out with the month of May.

When the sun came through the clouds people cautiously peeked out of the doorways up and down the street. Then, reassured by a warm wind, they began to come out of the buildings. Old men trudged out of the library and reclaimed their places on sidewalk benches where many of them, I imagine, had enjoyed twenty years of spring and summer afternoons. Children scrambled out of the school building where they had been held after three to keep them dry. A greengrocer in a white apron stepped out of his shop and started to fill his outdoor stand with squash, tomatoes, lettuce, and potatoes in their familiar rows of yellow, red, green, and brown.

Standing on the Portland street with puddles still everywhere, I felt glad to be here with everybody, glad to be part of the collective enterprise of human life. As I walked, my sneakers squished with each step. I felt really good and headed for home.

The next day I was out walking again, enjoying the spring.

I stopped at the local cigar store to pick up a paper, but found them out of stock. "Damn," I thought, "can't even get a paper after ten in the morning," continuing into town in search of a store. After walking several blocks I began to meditate on my breath, puffing on its going-in and comings-out like an old man puffs on a pipe. With each block I could feel my consciousness change, its normal humdrum preoccupations replaced by the keen awareness of meditation.

On the way home I saw an old woman walking slowly ahead of me. As my visual concentration came to rest on her I felt a deep, aching pain in my right hip and in both knees, as if they were, all of a sudden, swollen and blistered on the insides. I limped forward to catch up with the old woman. As we slowly made our way down the street, the woman told me she had arthritis in her hip and both legs. I knew this was true because *literally*, I could feel her pain. When she turned the corner and I looked away from her, my legs once again took on their springy and comfortable walk.

I did not take time out to think about this experience right away, as my mind was taken up with the logistical arrangements for a large vegetarian dinner I was planning for the Portland premies.

During this time I was on an unyeasted-bread kick. "Un-yeasted" is actually a misnomer for this fine kind of bread, as the leavening within it is derived not from packets of yeast but from the natural yeast in the air. In the vegetarian menu I was planning for our coming feast, unyeasted whole wheat bread figured prominently on the baked goods list.

The evening before the party, I mixed up the ingredients for my unyeasted favorite and set it in a warm place to rise overnight. The next day, when I got up, I went straight to the kitchen to check the bread's progress. When I lifted the damp cloth off the mixing bowl, I was delighted to see that the flat, brown pancake of flour and water I had left the night before was now a rounded mass of leavened dough. The yeast from the air had done its work.

I picked up the heavy bowl and walked over to the kitchen window to look at the day. A gentle breeze was ruffling in the curtains and the sunlight looked especially yellow and bright as it came through new small leaves of the maple tree beside the house. A bird chirped, sitting in the tree. It was the first week in May and spring was really here.

I set the bowl on the counter and scooped the dough up. Holding it made my hands tingle a little bit as I realized that the yeast had made the dough alive. I laughed slightly to myself and looked at the dough closely. If this dough is alive, then the air is alive, too. I took a deep breath and felt the same tingle of life as the air came inside my lungs.

I put the dough on my wooden cutting block and began to work on it, kneading it slowly. Shortly, I heard more chirping at the window. I got some birdseed from the pantry and sprinkled it on the ledge. When I returned to the bread several sparrows came to peck up the seeds and sing.

As I kneaded the bread the rhythmic motion in my back and arms made me feel relaxed and peaceful. I knew there would be plenty more of this peaceful time ahead of me today, stirring soup and watching the bread rise and bake. I settled myself in for a spell of thinking.

The main thing on my mind was my recent experience with the old arthritic woman and the other times when I had apparently gone beyond my ordinary bounds and briefly felt part of another person's life. As I thought over my experiences I remembered the first time I realized that I was a separate person—when I was in kindergarten and wished to look out of a classmate's eyes. I had closed my eyes and set my will on making the journey from inside me to inside her. Then I had opened my eyes and found myself stuck, tightly wedged within myself.

I had hated to accept this limitation, but I saw no way around it. Eventually I got to rather like being only one person, only me, Sophia. But now something, most likely meditation, was loosening the glue. Though my experiences could be thought of as spiritual eavesdropping, I didn't think I'd run into any problems about illegal wiretapping. I wasn't invading anybody's privacy, I was just learning how to tune in on a public access channel which wasn't normally in use. If Jung was right that people have a uniform mental functioning (allowing for certain differences in intelligence and background), then anybody could have the experiences of literal empathy I had had.

When I considered what the world would be like if everybody was evolved spiritually to the point where they could use this communication channel regularly, I imagined a community of saints. Then I remembered Rennie's remark that Knowledge could be the basis of a new kind of social movement. The *new* part of the Knowledge movement would not be the brilliant policies set forth by it, but the changing, evolving consciousness of the movement's members. Each new realization would be a rung in a ladder leading from our present world into a future, better one. Fine thoughts to make the bread rise.

In the middle of the day, Sandy, one of the men who lived in our monastic household, came into the kitchen. By this time the bread was in the oven and I was halfway through a pile of dirty dishes. Needing someone to dry the growing stack in the dish drainer, I handed him the towel and we started to talk.

"You know, Soph," he said, "when I was in Boston I went to see Bal Bhagwan Ji, Guru Maharaj Ji's brother who's in charge of the Astrodome festival. I told him about the lasers."

Sandy was an art student whose main interest was holographs, three-dimensional photographs made with lasers.

"Bal Bhagwan Ji said I should go to Houston and do some holographs for the festival. Apparently he wants to do a big spiritual exhibit in the convention hall next to the dome."

Houston. I thought it over looking at all of the unwashed

dishes. "It sounds great, Sandy." For a moment I imagined all the things one could do if one had the Astrodome. Then I smelled the bread baking in the oven and looked out the window. "But what about everything you are doing here in Portland?" I asked. Sandy had another two months to go in art school. He was very popular in our household and carried organizational responsibility in the premie community. Besides these school and church commitments, Sandy also had other reasons to stay in town. Unlike so many of the people I met in Portland, Sandy was a local boy. His widowed mother lived about thirty miles away off in the woods. "You have roots here," I said.

"Well, the way I figure it, I don't have a big name, so I'll probably never get another chance to do a large show like this. At least not while I'm young. Plus, I can do it with a spiritual theme. The people who come to the Astrodome to see it will understand my message much better than if it was in a museum where it would be viewed by the general public. Does that sound reasonable? That's what I told my teachers at school.

"But I'll tell you the truth, Sophia, I don't really care so much about that part of it. The real thing I feel is that I want to help the mission. It is really nice here in Portland, but I'm starting to feel I didn't just come into the world to do for myself. I want to do for others, too. And, really, the best thing I can think of to do for anybody is tell them about meditation. If we tell enough people about it, I'll bet we can change the world."

My unyeasted bread was a hit at the dinner party that night. Tracy had come up from Boston to visit. After the feasting was over, I found myself over dirty dishes again; this time I was drying and Tracy was up to her elbows in the suds.

"Sandy's going to Houston," I told Tracy.

"Yeah?" she said nonchalantly. "You should go, too."

We looked at each other seriously for a moment and then Tracy's impish look came over her. "You want to, don't you?" she said.

In the months Tracy and I had rooms next to each other at our old house on Waterville Street she had gotten to know me pretty well. "Yes," I answered, realizing for the first time that it was true.

I wrote a letter describing myself in glowing terms to DLM's personnel department at the headquarters in Denver. I said I had experience in writing, business, and food management. After a week, I got a phone call from a young woman at DLM in Denver. She told me that if I could go to Houston right away, I'd have a ground-floor opportunity, starting up a food-buying club for the festival staff. The terms of employment were exactly the same as I had in Portland. In exchange for my work I would receive room and board in one of the mission-run monastic houses.

Next, I started to settle my affairs in Portland and withdraw from my commitments to a summer job and autumn schooling. The festival was scheduled for November. I figured I'd be down South at least until then.

My first call was to Bryn Mawr. A young woman in the admissions office answered the phone and I told her I wanted to withdraw my application. Looking through my file, she said, "Oh, I remember you. Why do you want to withdraw? You are going to be accepted."

I briefly told her of my plans to go to Houston.

"But you'd make such a fine doctor," she said. (Did you hear the trumpets?) "I am fascinated by these spiritual movements. My little brother is in one of them. You know, I am a graduate student in social anthropology and I have done a great deal of thinking about the implications of Eastern thought on our action-oriented world."

"Really?" I said. "I'd be very interested to hear about your ideas. Tell me about your brother."

"My little brother used to be at Stanford; now he's shaved

his head and all he does all day is sit, crosslegged, staring, eyes drooping, at the wall. I think he wants to go to Japan now to see a *roggi*, I mean *rishi*.

"I asked him why, and he said, 'Sister, Buddha promised to return age to age until even grass was realized. I betray life if I do not take up this noble path.'

"I asked him about his former ambitions, marriage, money. When addressing these subjects I initially felt his tone was somewhat blasé. I wondered if in our family we had set his ambitions too high, and then he had become disappointed, frustrated, and rejected the past. However, I gradually formed a different impression. He seemed to have no bitterness, only detachment. I sensed he was feeling something meaningful, even profound. And this experience, whatever it was, was motivating his actions. Though I continue to be baffled by the directions his actions are taking. Shaving his head . . . quitting Stanford. It is all so alien to our society.

"So, Miss Collier, please tell me why *you* are joining this group. It is important for me to understand what young people are doing."

I smiled at this last remark. If this stiff-sounding lady at the admissions office had a younger brother in Stanford recently, she couldn't be thoroughly beyond the pale of that age-group herself. I ran my story down for her as I had done many times before, to explain why I was involved with DLM.

"Since I was very small," I began, "I have had many experiences which showed me that our normal waking consciousness is not the only way of looking at things. Neither is it the best way. According to our way of seeing, each person is separate from all other people, separate from nature and separate from God. From my experience this is a fundamentally mistaken impression. And not only is it wrong, it runs in diametric opposition to the course life—humanity —needs to follow if we are to survive. The reason is this: If every person is separate, it is morally correct for each person to try to gather everything to himself. However, in a limited and overpopulated world, this will not work. New forms of greater cooperation must be developed.

"But it is not enough to think intellectually, 'Sure, we all have to work together.' Instead, there must be a feeling of essential unity that pervades every level of a person's being, so that a person's natural reaction is not the 'territorial imperative,' but a cooperative instinct."

"Sounds good so far," she said. "But what is the means through which this transformation will occur?"

"Meditation, I believe, can be that catalyst."

"Meditation?" The woman started to laugh. "I have heard that the journey of a thousand miles starts with a single step. And that water, the softest thing, has worn canyons. But meditation versus immorality sounds like an everlasting war. The flesh is weak, Miss Collier, the flesh is weak."

"Okay, now listen, may I ask you a personal question?"

"Yes?"

"How old are you?"

"Twenty-eight," she replied.

"Have you ever been stoned?"

"You mean, smoked marihuana?"

"Right," I said.

"Well . . . uh . . . yes."

"Okay. When you smoke, after a few puffs there comes a point where you 'get off,' after which you are stoned. Your consciousness is completely different from the one moment before when you hadn't yet felt the dope's effects."

"So?"

"Meditation, from my experience, is like that," I explained. "It is like the alchemist's stone. Of course, sometimes when you are trying to meditate it doesn't work. You don't 'get off.' It isn't foolproof like dope."

"What sort of experiences have you had which lead you to believe meditation has this sort of alchemical power?"

I gave her some examples. I told her about the guard dog and some of the other things I have already mentioned.

"All right," she replied. "From what you have told me, your plan is to become a saint by the transformational qualities you attribute to the mystical experience of meditation. And it seems to be working for you. But you are looking at it on a larger scale. You see the need to reform the existing *weltanschauung* of all people. In order to do this, you must get other people to do meditation too. That is the purpose of your Astrodome festival?"

"Yes," I said.

"But herein lies the difficulty with your plan," she went on. "St. Thomas Aquinas said that people could become saints merely by wanting to. Your idea at least is more functional than that. You have something to aid the mere power of will, you have this meditation. But, as with Aquinas, you also face the problem of will. If a person has no desire to transform his consciousness and improve his moral nature. . . . I, for instance, have never yearned for sainthood."

"So forget about sainthood," I said. "How about a little peace of mind? Would you like that?"

"Oh, I see. For those who are not attracted by humanitarian virtues, you hope to attract people through their more selfish motives. Very much like the TM ads I see around campus. They claim 'increased creative intelligence,' 'relaxation,' everything but a better sex life. And then, once you have hooked them on the practice of meditation, they will improve spiritually and morally. Well, this is very ambitious. I share your excitement. But I will put your application back in our file. I do not believe our age is ripe for the sort of thing to which you aspire. And one other thing, your leader—is he the young one? The one in his teens?"

"Sure. Guru Maharaj Ji."

"I think I saw him on television. And I am sorry to say, though you sound like an intelligent young woman, a woman who'd make a fine doctor, I found your leader, well, less than attractive. Please don't be offended."

The woman wished me luck and we said goodbye, she

wondering why I was giving my time to such a dubious prospectus for world peace and I wondering why such an insightful woman was not more interested in the new frontiers of consciousness.

The next call I made was to the director of the camp I had gone to as a child. She had hired me for the summer to build a sailboat. I had more or less talked her into the job, so when I called and said I wasn't going to do it, she was very surprised. The conversation was brief. I hung up feeling sorry that I hadn't been able to share more with someone I cared about so much.

In another week I was ready to go. Since the first day I had thought of going to Houston I had been in close communication with my mother. When I called her and said I was ready to leave Maine, she asked me one thing. "Have you become enlightened? I know you always wanted to be."

Confessing my lack in this regard, I told her I would call once I got to Houston. This was, in her opinion, one of the less wild ideas I had come up with on how to spend the summer. After a month she came to visit me in Houston. Staying several weeks, she helped me with the laundry and bought me and my DLM friends large quantities of ice cream in a suitable motherly way.

As you may have noticed by now, I had a very positive outlook, but I knew a more serious involvement in DLM wouldn't be all roses. I knew that Divine Light Mission would need a lot of work in order to get into fighting shape. The mission's biggest problem wasn't hard to miss—it was the overwhelming Indian influence pervading the entire organization. The least dangerous way this influence was exerted was in the Indians' predilection for things which struck me as tasteless and gaudy. Their tinsel garlands and crowns for the young guru were not my idea of haute couture. I did not share their enthusiasm for rooms whose primary decoration was a huge altar with pictures of the "holy family," Guru Maharaj Ji and his kin. If given my way, my tastes run to a room full of pre-Victorian handmade antiques with Chinese rugs on the floor, a Ming vase holding flowers, and some Paul Klees on the wall.

Naturally I do not expect everyone to go my way on matters of decor, but decor was not where the Indian influence ended. As mahatmas, or close disciples of Guru Maharaj Ji, they felt they had a certain authority which they could use to spread their views on every subject. Since few of them were actually renaissance men or women—people with a wide understanding and education in the arts and sciences—the opinions expressed by the Indian faction were rarely the last word on any subject. More often the ideas were simply Indian folklore, quotes from the scriptures, prejudices from their place in the class structure of Indian culture, misinformation, Indian nationalism, or Indian mythology applied to modern situations.

One thing that amused me and many of the Western premies was the Indian fascination with systems of numeration. I have heard mahatmas expound with great authority on: The Nine Grievous Errors, The Four Graces, The Eight Million Four Hundred Thousand Forms of Living Things, The Sixty-Four Powers of the Guru, and the Five Manifestations of the Satguru. This last one was a particularly potent and popular idea. And, as far as I can tell, it is one of the few bits of original cosmology developed by DLM in India.

Most of the mahatmas were of the opinion that not only was Maharaj Ji divine himself, but so were the four other members of his family. I think it was Mata, Guru Maharaj Ji's mother, who came up with this idea and then spread it around. In this scheme, Mata embodied the compassionate characteristics of God. She was the Holy Mother, Mother of Creation. Bal Bhagwan Ji, the eldest brother, embodied wisdom and intellect. Bhole Ji, the next brother, embodied art and music. (This was a singularly unappealing idea, because Bhole Ji's appearance and speech were not very graceful. Believers in the "five fingers of God" idea, ever inventing ways to patch up leaks in their cosmology, excused his lack of aesthetic appeal by saying Bhole Ji "hadn't gotten out of his deep meditation yet.") Raja Ji, the third brother, was supposed to embody courage or the qualities of statesmanship. In the future world the mahatmas envisioned, Raja Ji was the King.

To offset all the bad taste and the fascination with numbers, the mahatmas did have one redeeming social value that made their other qualities tolerable, at least in my mind. The mahatmas did understand, after all, that Knowledge worked. Their complex other ideas concerned the explanation behind the experience. Even if all of their explanations were just crazy mumbo-jumbo, they had understood the most important part about Knowledge well enough to teach it to me, to help me open the door into my own inner world. A similar situation might be found among the early medicine people of Europe and Asia. They used the flowered plant we call foxglove to treat certain kinds of illnesses. The folklore abounded with the how and why behind the healing power of this pretty purple-flowered plant—all of which we think of as incorrect; in fact, we regard foxglove as a dangerous poison. Those early medicine people did not know that foxglove could cure because it contains digitalis, as scientists now believe.

Just as I respect the administrators of foxglove for what they knew, I respected the mahatmas for their Knowledge. Beyond this I admired their dedication. They were not paid, receiving only expenses in exchange for their work; but still they continued to travel and teach people the one really great thing they knew.

With eyes wide open to all of the potentials and problems, I got on the plane and went to Houston. When I arrived I scanned the faces of the crowd for the right smile. I didn't have any idea who would be picking me up. When the crowd of people thinned out I saw a nice-looking young man with a Maharaj Ji button on. He drove me from the airport and showed me to my new accommodations. They turned out to be a lovely little place on the floor where I could put my sleeping bag. Not exactly the Plaza.

I have a theory that at people's birth they are endowed with a certain amount of "put up." Because young people still have an ample supply of this valuable commodity, they can put up with more than older people. At seventeen I still had plenty of put up left, so a sleeping bag on the floor and a little place in the closet to hang up "everything I owned" seemed fine and dandy to me. I shared this room with three other women who, fortunately, were pleasant people without any odd habits.

After a day's rest I went to the festival offices to see one of the principal organizers and learn about my new job. I was to organize a buying club to serve the eating needs of the thirty-five staff members who were presently in Houston, and then gradually expand its capacity as the staff grew. Eventually the "co-op" would be serving the several-thousand-member staff at festival time. Another person, a bright fellow named Peter, was also going to work with me building this accordion-like co-op.

Peter and I got along immediately. I felt he had a rare and valuable character, and insight into life. Twelve years older than I, he had traveled all over the world and met many fascinating people. He was originally from Long Island and had an M.A. in English Literature. Traveling around in the red VW bus we had been given to use for the food business, we had many lively talks about subjects ranging from the works of Shakespeare and Sartre to the worth of Buddhism and bisexuality.

We loved what we were doing. Peter had been working in a large food co-op in Boston before he came to Houston. He thought of co-ops as a mutual aid philosophy made practical. Our present job of feeding our large spiritual "family" was to him a dream realized. We worked very hard, often getting up before dawn and driving far out of town to the farmers' market to buy the best produce. Because of our demonstrated ability to get things done, the houseparents asked us to buy all of their household goods as well as the food.

Then, in some stroke of management brilliance, Peter and Sophia, the wonder kids, suddenly were put in charge of laundry, plus food and the other services we were already providing. Of the two of us, Peter and me, guess who got to do the wash. Right. Me. The same credential that had recommended me in Portland—my amazing ability to operate a washing machine—was now recommending me in Houston.

Peter was too good of a pal to abandon me to a pile of dirty laundry. Until I got another assistant, he helped me quite a bit. Together we sorted the clothes at the beginning of the day. Then he would go off on his errands, buying food. At the end of the day he returned to help fold.

Our days were very long, but it didn't bother me. In fact, I somewhat enjoyed going to bed tired for a change. Throughout my life I have always been a very energetic person. Once when I was nine, after running around the outside of the house a few times, I badgered my father for something to do. He suggested I turn one hundred cartwheels. When I finished doing that I was not satisfied, so I decided to stand the other way and turn one hundred more.

In the laundry I met a cross section of the Houston population. I met an honest-to-God bank robber, who shortly afterward was caught and thrown in the slammer. I met a former IBM executive who was getting away from it all, working as a dry-cleaning counterman. Then there was a midget who fell in love with me. And a Spanish woman with *sixteen* children; a black mother on welfare; assorted wealthy young bachelors, who, incidentally, didn't have the amazing ability to operate a washing machine.

Hanging around the laundromat all day, I heard a lot of stories. I couldn't help but be moved by many of the people who came into the "mat," dragging their laundry, and then sitting down to sweat while the clothes washed and dried in the Houston summer.

Some of the premies at the festival offices put out a small newsletter about the activities and progress of the festival plans. To spruce up this Xeroxed rag, occasionally they included a story or poem. In the lull between "wash" and "spin" I couldn't resist writing about the mat and the people I met there. After a few of my vignettes had been published, Diana Stone, a premie who was coordinating some of the PR for the festival, called me.

"You're an artist," she told me. "You should come up here and work with me. Write stuff for the *Divine Times*, for our leaflets."

And so I was delivered from the laundry.

When I told my laundromat friends that I was leaving, they all were glad for me. The woman with sixteen children told me, "Listen, it isn't often a laundress gets a chance to write for a newspaper."

Or a writer gets a chance to spend a month in a laundromat, I thought to myself.

It was around this time that I met Guru Maharaj Ji. He had recently arrived in the United States from India and was stopping over in Houston on his way somewhere else. The dance troupe which was to perform at the festival had also arrived, and had arranged an audience with him. Since I had never met my guru before, one of the dancers suggested that I come along. We gathered in the large room where we had our evening lectures, and waited. And waited. In the three years I was involved with DLM, I only heard of one occasion when Maharaj Ji arrived at a meeting or program on time. I believe Maharaj Ji came late on purpose to create a mood of anticipation, but not so late as to make anyone really mad. After forty-five minutes he pulled up in a Mercedes-Benz and jumped out like a dapper star arriving on a movie set. He looked great—shiny, clean, and cheerful. He was wearing a nice suit. His jet-black hair was fashionably long and accented his strong, dark eyes. He wasn't as fat as people said.

Once he was in the room, he wouldn't sit down; instead he stood and chatted informally. The dancers had some business questions they wanted to ask, but he would have nothing of it. He ignored their attempts to be serious, making jokes, laughing, and telling them how much he liked their dancing. Throughout his good-natured conversation there was something of the stern father in his voice, mixed in with the more obvious sound of a mischievous playmate. It struck me that he was a subversive character along the lines of Dr. Seuss's Cat in the Hat.

Gradually, I felt myself becoming completely intoxicated. I felt very close to Maharaj Ji and the dancers who were present. As in a romantic novel, everything got "kinda misty," and I felt like I was falling in love in a general way with the whole world.

Upon seeing Maharaj Ji, I did not collapse into a sobbing pool of tears as Baba Ram Dass reports having done upon meeting his Maharaj Ji, an older, more traditional guru. But I definitely felt a warm glow. I liked him.

12

As a writer, I had much more pleasant working conditions than I had labored under as a laundress. Instead of a
sweaty "washateria," as they call laundromats in Houston,
I now was given a nice air-conditioned office on a quiet street
with a window overlooking a full-blossomed magnolia tree.
My standing assignment was to write about the progress of
the Millennium festival preparations for the *Divine Times.*
I could write anything I wanted to, with the tacit understanding that it would portray Guru Maharaj Ji, DLM, and
the coming festival in a favorable light.

The way I planned to approach my position as propagandist was to examine whatever I saw as negative in the organization by severely confronting whoever was perpetrating
the problem. I would weigh what I learned against my sense
of DLM's overall worth. Since I had a high opinion of
DLM's potential, I assumed it would take something pretty
atrocious to make me arrive at a negative net worth by this
analysis. Then, if the item was newsworthy, I planned to
present the facts accompanied by the context I saw, and the
reader could make up his own mind, in the light of his own
opinion of DLM's overall worth. I believed DLM's strength
would be drawn from informed and committed members
who each were certain in their reasons for alliance.

By following this plan, I believed I would never have to
compromise myself. In a situation where I looked at the assets

and liabilities of the organization and saw a negative net worth, I thought, knowing me, I wouldn't hang around too long. First chance I got, I'd be down at the airlines office, making reservations to go home.

Pad and pencil in hand, I set out to do my first article: a study of the way the Houston festival staffers lived when they were off the job. I thought this would be interesting, as it would include short portraits of a few of the staff members with more varied backgrounds—Peter and his travels through Asia, for instance.

In the course of preparing the article I spoke with one of the festival organizers and mentioned the disorganized manner in which medical care was handled. He seemed genuinely surprised that I saw a problem.

"Well, it may not be so together now. You know we are sort of low on cash, but after Millennium we won't have to worry about anything."

"Oh, really, why not?" I said, expecting to hear that DLM was getting a national health insurance policy. Or starting a clinic with premie doctors while financing interested ashram residents through medical school.

He looked at me with sympathy, as if I were hopelessly uninformed. "Because," he said, "after the festival is the New Age."

"Come on," I replied. "When we decided to call the festival 'Millennium' I thought it was because our vision of one peaceful world based on spiritual values was evoked by the word, 'Millennium'—not because the hoped-for Millennium will begin on November eighth, the day we take over the Dome. You heard Bob say that," I concluded, referring to a recent meeting we had both attended with Bob Mishler, the DLM president.

"That's not what Bal Bhagwan Ji says," the fellow continued; but, seeing my skepticism, he demurred, "Who knows what will happen?" He shrugged and smiled.

The New Age. It signifies a complete transformation of

the world as we know it, into another perfect world where all manner of evil and suffering have passed away. People from every sort of background believe the New Age will come, but their ideas vary greatly on the "how" behind its arrival.

Some—the "have you read Revelations?" crowd—believe a horrible binge of physical destruction will obliterate the present world with all of its sinning inhabitants and quickly replace it with a perfect one. Perhaps, they speculate, God will come out of the clouds on a golden chariot and orchestrate the end.

Others—like Anne Frank, the sweet little girl who wrote in her diary after seeing some of her family shot to death by Nazis, "I still believe that people are basically good at heart"—believe it will just happen. People's higher nature will get the best of them.

Then, there are those people who believe that the New Age is inevitable, but it is going to take time and bucks, blood and sweat. (Count me in here, though there's a little of the second group in me, too.)

Even within these three groups, people's timetables vary. There is little agreement just when the awaited hour will dawn. Dr. Laurence Peter—in the Anne Frank group—feels it will be in the next twenty years or so. He discusses how, when, and where at length in his book, *The Peter Plan*.

Cesar Chavez—in the time and bucks group—has a simpler analysis and expectation. "You want to know what I really think?" he says. "I really think one day the world will be great."

But the most interesting timetable for the arrival of the New Age is envisioned by the Jehovah's Witnesses. The New Age, they say, is already here. It came sometime in the early part of the century, when Christ quietly returned to earth.

Whatever is the case about the New Age, it seemed to have little relevance to my *Divine Times* article. Using another person's comment on premie health care, I finished my article and sent it to Denver, where the newspaper's editorial offices were located. But this was not the last time I heard of an unfounded thing that "Bal Bhagwan Ji said."

"New York is going to have earthquakes in October!" someone was yelling outside my door. "Bal Bhagwan Ji says the fault runs right down Fourteenth Street!"

Well, that's one way to get rid of the old S. Klein building, I thought, remembering a particular eyesore in the Fourteenth Street area. From what I could determine from the conversation in the hall, the belief of Bal Bhagwan Ji—or BB, as I shall affectionately call him—in New York's rumbling demise was not founded on any studies of the terrain in that area. Even though some mahatmas considered BB to be the embodiment of intellect and wisdom, in making this prediction he had no seismographs at his disposal. No experts had advised him. It was something that just occurred to him one day. It was "revealed truth," like the Bible's Book of Revelations.

Because Bal Bhagwan Ji was not in Houston at the time, we got wind of his idea through other premies. Most of the people only repeated BB's ideas out of surprise and astonishment, but some premies actually believed what BB was saying.

Peter and I and some of our other friends started calling these people who picked up on BB's ideas *Victims of the Millennium Fever*. Implicit in this description was our conviction that eventually their symptoms would go away: a fever eventually breaks and the victims return to their former healthy selves. Fortunately, even at the peak of contagion, the fever was limited to a minority of premies, mostly in Houston.

In reflecting on the Millennium Fever from the vantage of four years, there is one thing which particularly strikes me. I find it curious that it is so easy for people to feel identified with a spiritual organization even when they have considerable differences of opinion with the leadership. As I live and see more of the world, I realize this is common to all spiritual organizations.

For instance, Catholicism. People call themselves Catholics for many reasons. The Pope, who is acknowledged as the head of the Roman Catholic religion, has spoken out strongly against birth control and even more harshly against abortion. But this does not mean that all Catholics feel this way. The other day I heard that a doctor in charge of a large abortion clinic in Florida said 40 percent of the women who come into his clinic for abortions are practicing Catholics. This is a very interesting figure, when you consider that only 20 percent of the Florida population in that area is Catholic.

From what I understand of the Catholic spiritual organization, papal authority is one of the most basic tenets. Yet these people are willing to go against what the Pope has specifically said and still consider themselves part of the Catholic community.

Catholics who have had abortions are tied to the faith by something deeper and more important to them than any rules, dogma, or creed. (I will not speculate on just *what* it is that creates this strong bond. Suffice to say that it exists and exerts strong power in a person's life.)

In the same way, acknowledgment of the common bond which attracted each of us to DLM made it easy for premies with differences of opinion to coexist. When I sat in early morning group meditation, I was moved to respect the other premies, even those with Millennium Fever, because I felt our common urge toward higher awareness and a new world.

I remember one particular morning when I was getting ready to meditate with a group of about forty others. Since we wanted to get a good jump on the day, we generally started meditating at about 5:00 A.M. At this time it was still dark outside; gradually, during the hour we sat together in meditation, the sky grew light.

On this morning we were sitting in a circle and I could

see the face of nearly every person there. After about half an hour I opened my eyes. I felt very peaceful and I looked around at the meditators.

Some of the people I could see were stretching and straining to concentrate; their brows were slightly furrowed like those of students studying weighty texts. Others were calm; they had almost baby-like faces, the faces of angels, I thought. A carpenter I didn't like very much had a small smile. His rough hands rested in his lap. Several people were nodding, falling asleep for an instant but firmly waking themselves up again and again. Looking at these sleepy ones, I recognized our housemother. I knew she had been up late the previous night making lunches. I felt a little rush of inspiration as I saw her effort.

Sitting there that morning I experienced the bond the people in DLM shared. It was our common hope, our common effort to meet and merge with that vast interior world and then, in whatever way, to bring that profound inner grace to life in the outer world of action.

I felt like a person on a frontier, bonded to my fellow travelers by our common desire to get to the other side. With this feeling of community established inside me, it was hard to judge, but easy to forgive, what I saw as temporary troubles and aberrations in my friends' spirits.

But I hardly knew Bal Bhagwan Ji. He was not a friend whose deep intentions I trusted and understood. If the premies I knew who repeated his odd ideas were victims of Millennium Fever, BB was the Fever's carrier.

By the time BB arrived in Houston I had pieced together his whole prophetic scheme. All of BB's ideas had one central focus: the festival we were planning for November would be "the most holy and significant event in human history." It would not be a private great event—an Astrodome official told me that every religious group which has a gathering there secretly believes the dome was built for them—*everyone* would know.

Between the present time and the time of the festival, according to BB's predictions, there would be a series of major disasters, natural and political. To augment this there would also be a series of extraterrestrial phenomena. (Remember Kohoutek comet and the frequent UFO sightings of the summer of '73?) All of these things would lead people to seek the return of the messiah. Since BB was a scripture freak, he had dug up these qualifications for The Coming One.

From the prophet Isaiah, for instance:

The wolf also shall dwell with the lamb, and the
leopard shall lie down with the kid; and the calf
and the young lion and the fatling together; and a
little child shall lead them. They shall not hurt
nor destroy in all my holy mountain: for the earth
shall be full of the Knowledge of the Lord, as the
waters cover the sea.

Or this one, from a Tibetan source:

The sun and the moon dance and blow the trumpets,
and a *little child* shall turn the Wheel of the Law.
Secret of the body, of the Word and Heart of God,
His innermost breath is the steed of the Bodhisattvas.

When considering a "little child" for the role, BB's mind naturally went to the one little child he knew best—his own kid brother, Guru Maharaj Ji *aka* The Lord. The Millennium festival was the event at which the world would find out what BB already knew.

I was anxious to speak to BB and see if I really could be a propagandist with honor. It soon became clear, however, that an interview with BB was hard to come by. He was a very busy man. Or so everyone said. From the first he had taken a great interest in the festival, and sometime in the early summer Maharaj Ji had put him "in charge" of the festival effort. Despite the title though, it was commonly understood that Rennie Davis, going under the more humble

157

billing of "General Coordinator," was the person to listen to on any nuts and bolts issues involving the event.

Finally, after trying to see BB for several weeks, I gave up and started working on other things. Then, suddenly, BB wanted to see me; not because he wished to make known why he believed as he did, but instead because he had discovered my background in food service.

I arrived at the scheduled hour, but was told to wait outside: BB was not yet ready to see me. After a half-hour the door to BB's room opened a crack and a hand motioned me to enter. (Maharaj Ji and all the members of his family posted sentries at their doors to regulate the stream of devotees who came to seek their advice, counsel, or blessings.) Entering the room I saw several of the festival brass sitting on the floor. BB, himself, was seated comfortably on a chair with his feet resting on a cushion. He wore white traditional Indian garments—a dhoti and kirta. His chair was white, the cushion was white, and the rug was white. It was a rather dramatic effect, the highlight of which were BB's deep black eyes and black moustache.

Rennie Davis suddenly entered the room. "Hey, Rennie!" I greeted my friend, in what I later was informed was a serious breach of protocol. Rennie undoubtedly heard me, but did not respond. Instead he went straight to BB and bowed deeply as Christians sometimes do before the cross. After acknowledging Rennie with a loving smile, BB then looked at me.

I had no feeling of reverence or humility in front of this young Indian, so I kind of cocked my head and said hello without bowing. After an awkward pause, I was introduced. BB studied me for a moment and then, speaking quickly, asked, "How many have you cooked for?"

"Well, two twenty-five," I estimated.

"How many work in the kitchen?"

"Sometimes just me," I answered, "but if you set it up right you'd have four. Two main cooks. A dishwasher. And a pot washer who'd double as a veggie chopper . . ." I continued detailing my idea of a good cooking setup.

In the middle of my presentation he nodded as if I had said enough. "In *our* kitchen," he said, "two hundred and twenty-five will *work*. *Thousands* and thousands will be fed."

"Oh, really?" I raised my eyebrows. "Where will this be?"

"Here in this city, in Houston. Many will be coming, you know." He spoke with authority. The people seated on the floor noted all of this down in small notebooks.

After a few more questions, BB appeared to lose interest in me and began to expound a theory he had developed about Kohoutek comet and UFOs. "The stock market will fall in October." (I wondered if this would correspond with the predicted earthquake.) "And at least 400,000 people will be at our November Millennium."

All of this was respectfully noted.

Hoping nobody would notice, I quietly left the room. Walking home, I found I had a bad headache. The thing that bothered me the most was not BB's ideas, but the respect with which Rennie and the others listened to him. I knew that even though BB claimed 400,000 (or 200,000, depending on the day) would come to the festival and Rennie carefully noted this down as if he believed BB, Rennie would then quietly reserve hotel rooms for only 22,000.

"From my tours to promote the festival and my previous experience organizing this sort of event, I know 22,000 is all we can count on. It's a reasonable figure," I had heard Rennie remark a few days before. "If others come," Rennie continued almost whimsically, "it will be the grace of God, so then the grace of God can house them, too."

Why was Rennie leading BB on in this way? The whole situation started to smell like power politics. BB's lack of proportion was evident, but as brother of the guru, he couldn't be put out to pasture in the same way as a less nobly born leader. Historically, the less gifted relatives of the monarch are a common problem for royalty.

It must have been clear to Maharaj Ji when he arrived in the United States in late June 1973 that BB was treading on thin ice. Why did he leave BB in charge of the Astrodome festival? In order to make sense of this, I had to consider Maharaj Ji's position on a global basis.

He was "the Guru" for a constituency that numbered over one million. Many members of this group lived in India and shared, at least to some extent, the mahatmas' idea of the Hans family as five forms of a single divinity. Even though Maharaj Ji recognized this penta-god idea as rubbish, it was something he inherited with the mission. When at the age of eight he accepted the post, he took with it the whole shebang. So even though Maharaj Ji had been gradually working away at the accumulated religious concepts of the followers he inherited with the mission, he didn't want to do anything too radical which would send his Indian devotees packing down the street to the local swami.

Even if Maharaj Ji wanted to stage a little cultural revolution in the mission, he knew he couldn't do it just yet. His mother had worked long and hard at achieving a strong power base in India. The followers of her late husband, Hans, had naturally looked to her for wisdom during the period when Maharaj Ji was a small boy-guru. She would crush any challenge to her power.

The first time I saw Mata was at an airport reception in Houston. I did not like her at all. About a hundred or so people bringing garlands and flowers had come to meet her. As she came down the airport hall, I saw that she was quite fat. Her skin and hair had a greasy shine. Bundled up in a silk sari, she hurried past the people who had come to greet her. When she turned to look at someone, I saw the distinctive flash of a diamond in her nose.

People thrust the flowers toward her and she took them up with her pudgy hands, often breaking and crushing them in the process. In a moment she was gone. I was disappointed because I had hoped to like her, at least a little.

During her years of spiritual dominance, Mata had managed to advance her position in the spiritual hierarchy. Very much like Shri Aurobindo's wife, who took over Aurobindo's mission after his death, Mata became DLM's patron. She traveled everywhere with little Maharaj Ji, speaking before he did, telling stories she had heard from Hans.

In my opinion, Mata was a traditional Hindu. To her, DLM was a family business. A shrewd businessperson, Mata set out to solidify her power base, until eventually, as Bob Mishler told me, "She had India wrapped up like a spiritual Mafia."

What Mata did not count on was that her son, Maharaj Ji, the main capital in her business, would not want to go along with her scheme. It wasn't public knowledge at this point that the members of the family did not get along, but word filtered out from the people who lived with the Hans family that they were fighting more and more. The sides in these fights were clear from the beginning. It was Mata, BB, and Bhole Ji who were carrying the flag for traditional Indian culture against Maharaj Ji and Raja Ji, who wanted to throw out the old ways and get into the Western world to create a new kind of spirituality.

The pathetic thing about this struggle was that it did not come into the open until much later. It was the kind of cruel and private fight that only families can have. Publicly, the five stood together and smiled as if, as one journalist wrote, "God is in his Astrodome and all is right with the world." Perhaps Maharaj Ji hoped things would somehow resolve themselves and he would not have to take that most painful step of renouncing his family and splitting up the mission his father and he had worked so hard to build.

In the light of these background forces, the question of why Maharaj Ji left BB in charge of the festival had a simple answer. Guru Maharaj Ji was up against the wall. If he fired BB, those Indian devotees who thought of the family as being five forms of the same divinity might find this violated their ideas, and might leave the mission altogether. If he tried to push BB into the background—keeping BB around but in a minor position—it would offend Mata-BB-Bhole Ji's high sense of their own importance and would make them retaliate. If all else failed, Mata could fall back on the traditional way mothers control their children. "Don't forget you are underage, dear."

If BB was the only thing Maharaj Ji had to worry about, then, I concluded, Maharaj Ji actually would not be facing a major problem. The kinds of predictions BB was making were like bonds that mature quickly. Everything he was predicting was to happen within 90 to 120 days. He said the stock market would fall in October. When, on November first, people were still scurrying around on the Wall Street trading floor, he would be discredited. He said 400,000 people would come to Millennium; when only 22,000 showed up, again, he'd be discredited. From a PR point of view, BB was digging his own grave.

However, because of Maharaj Ji's stand-and-smile-with-the-family policy, I thought Maharaj Ji might fall into BB's grave too. Rennie and other prominent figures in DLM were very busy inviting the press to see the festival. How could a journalist resist reporting what the Millennium Fever victims were saying?

Sitting and considering these things in my cool office overlooking the magnolia tree, I kept wondering what Maharaj Ji would do. That fifteen-year-old kid has got some pretty deft maneuvering in front of him if he is going to pull out of this alive, I thought, feeling glad I had friends, not followers, and parents without vested interest in how I lived. I was not the least bit surprised when Maharaj Ji came down with an ulcer.

That summer Maharaj Ji had been touring the United States and Europe. From what I could see, Maharaj Ji's style of "leadership" was to leave all of the nitty-gritty decisions about DLM operations to the headquarters in Denver, while dividing his own time between giving lectures for the membership or the public and "resting," a euphemism for his long periods of inactivity. At his speaking engagements he rarely spoke about the organization, but rather concentrated on subjects with which he was more familiar, like meditation and Knowledge.

His itinerary was packed for the summer's tour. He had public programs in several major cities, TV appearances, and some appointments to receive awards and keys to various cities, as well as more intimate premie programs for the membership only. Things were going well until he got to Detroit, where he was to receive a civic citation. After he accepted the award, an underground-newspaper reporter came rushing up to Maharaj Ji and, in what the reporter described as "a protest against God," hit Maharaj Ji in the face with a shaving cream pie. This in itself was not a tragedy. But what happened afterward was.

Two premies sought out the pie-thrower, Pat Halley, and creamed him with a steel pipe. This was a dreadful and pathetic example of fanaticism at work. What makes it worse is that I know, from a very good source, that one of the premie assailants was a mahatma, a DLM figure who initiated many thousands of U.S. premies in 1971–1973. Maharaj Ji did not know of this mahatma's plans beforehand, and afterward when the incident came to his attention Maharaj Ji stripped the mahatma of his rank and urged him to turn himself in to the police. However, the mahatma did not follow this advice and quietly slipped out of the country. The other assailant, Bob Mishler believes, was an American and still even today lives in a DLM ashram. If this is true I feel Maharaj Ji is at fault. He should have pursued this matter more aggressively and made sure the perpetrators were apprehended and tried in a court of law.

One day, as I was thinking about these things, I went out

to buy a candy bar. A man standing in line at the cash register noticed my "Who Is Guru Maharaj Ji?" button and asked, "Well, okay, who is he?"

Before I had a chance to launch into the rap I had developed, the man whipped out a card and handed it to me. "Ed Krotin, Imperial Wizard, Ku Klux Klan," was embossed on it.

"Klan, huh?" I said sweetly. "Do you still bomb Negro churches?"

"Only when they need it. We don't need you in Houston," he hissed, and left without paying for his large cigar.

Chewing on my Hershey bar, it occurred to me that I'd just met someone like the pipe-wielding mahatma.

CHAPTER

13

"YOU GUYS ARE A BUNCH OF GODDAMN FANATICS. YOU'RE GOING to ruin this festival with your bongo ideas."

I whirled around to see who had said this, the most sensible thing I had heard in weeks. The speaker appeared to be a skinny teen-aged boy, but upon a second look I realized it was a young woman, maybe twenty-two or twenty-three. "Who's that?" I asked a person standing next to me.

"Oh, that's Lola Jackson. She's in charge of Soul Rush." Soul Rush. I'd been hearing about it for quite a while, but I was never sure it would get off the ground. The idea behind Soul Rush was to have a traveling show that would tour several major cities to promote the festival in Houston. The show would consist of three parts: in the late morning, a colorful parade peopled with local premies and the 500-member Soul Rush staff (who would be following the tour route in buses); in the afternoon, a one-act musical created by a small Boston theater company; and in the evening, a three-hour rock-and-roll performance by Blue Aquarius, a fifty-five-piece band that brought together all of the big name premie musicians. All of this would be put on for free.

Seeing the vast amount of energy and money that was needed in Houston, I thought it was unlikely that the Soul Rush tour would ever get rolling. But now, right here in the Millennium offices' lunchroom, was a sensible-sounding young woman trying to pull it together.

The person standing next to me filled me in on Lola's past activities in DLM. "She was general secretary in Boulder for a year. The only woman local director at that time. She's also the only ashram resident who Maharaj Ji told to go to college. She's smart and a good friend of Bob Mishler's . . ."

Well, it always helps to have friends in high places, I thought, tuning in on Lola's conversation again.

"Bob and I are together on this," Lola said in no uncertain terms. "Soul Rush is going to be run cash-on-the-barrel. No credit for us. You can run this Houston scene any way you want to, but when I'm running the show, we do it my way: cash."

The credit arrangements for the festival had troubled me. A friend in the "finance" department told me that we already owed $230,000—and it was only July. Our debts were not long-term notes, either; everything came due right after the festival. If there was ever an unsound financial plan, this was it.

The person to whom Lola was speaking immediately recognized her authority. "Of course you are right, but only for Soul Rush." He began to defend the Millennium office's credit arrangements. "When a tour comes through town, it's there maybe for a day; then it leaves, and people forget. They are not going to give money later. But Millennium is going to be big, really big. People will give us the money afterward. Bal Bhagwan Ji said . . ."

Lola seemed to bristle at the mention of BB. "You don't know that," she interrupted. "If you can't get the money now, there isn't much reason to believe you'll be able to get the money then." Lola looked at her watch. "I have to go now. I've got a meeting and then I'm flying up to Boston. We're setting up our offices there."

"I wonder if there are any openings on the Soul Rush staff," I asked the person with whom I had been speaking before I saw Lola.

"I don't know, but I think Lola's leaving this evening.

Why don't you go see Susan Gregory? She'll be here a few weeks tying things up before going to Boston herself."

I'd met Susan Gregory before. She was Rennie's old partner from the peace movement. One of Diana Stone's first writing ideas for me was a profile of Susan, focussing on the theme, "What are the New Left leaders of the Sixties up to now?" The article never came through, but I had several long talks with Susan while preparing it. We liked each other.

"I love the idea of this tour—how can I get on the staff?" was my first question.

"Maybe you can do the Soul Rushers' laundry," she teased me. Then, "This is politics," she said, her tone more serious. "I know the personnel department in Denver is going to assign someone, but it probably won't be you. It will be someone they know better . . ."

"But you know me," I protested, reminding her of our two-week association.

Susan smiled and then answered, "You get to Boston without getting kicked out of the ashram and we'll put you to work."

If the personnel department was already in the process of assigning someone to Soul Rush, I knew I'd have to act quickly. I knew of a ride going north, almost to Massachusetts.

With my yippie moxie still intact, I walked past the secretary into the middle of a high-level meeting in Rennie's office. "Rennie," I spoke very fast, "I can save the mission two hundred dollars if I go to Boston now, rather than wait until later. I know of a ride, but I have to leave right now."

Rennie looked at me blankly. "Oh . . . sure, good. Go to Boston. I give you my okay." It never occurred to him that I hadn't even been assigned to Soul Rush.

Boston Debs See The Light was the headline in the society section of the *Boston Globe* the day I arrived in Boston. Poss, my old friend from Maine, showed me the newspaper at the

Divine Sales store, a secondhand outlet he ran for the mission in Boston.

"Well, Poss, you finally got to live in a real ashram," I said, remembering how much he used to talk about the value of monastic life when we both lived in our commune in Portland. As we talked, we relaxed on an old couch outside the store and waited for my ride to the Soul Rush offices in another part of the city. Springs popped up out of the couch's cushions on either side of Poss's knees. Around us were the day's "bargains": racks of old clothes, furniture that matched the couch if not in styling then in repair, and an old mirror.

Inside the store, premies were haggling over prices with customers and running after street children who were forever finding their way into places they shouldn't be. "Hey! Hey!" we heard behind us. One child was now standing on top of an old oak dresser. "I'm Superfly!" he shouted, leaping to the ground.

"This place is really some scene," I said, noticing that Diana Stone, the woman who rescued me from the laundromat in Houston, was coming down the street.

"Wow, it's a celebrity," Poss said, pointing out that Diana, originally from Boston, was one of the "debs" mentioned in the *Globe*'s article.

"What are you doing in town?" Diana and I asked each other at the same time.

We swapped stories. She was here as part of a fund-raising tour, "visiting millionaires." Diana had an almost inbred feel for the business of tact and cultured salesmanship. Her father was a high-ranking official in the U.S. State Department. Throughout her childhood, Diana had traveled with her family to many parts of the world while her father represented the United States. When she joined DLM, she was living in India with her parents. News of her conversion spread quickly.

"It didn't take long before all of the diplomats in New

Delhi knew that the daughter of the American chargé d'affaires was into some young guru," Diana related. "An Italian told me, 'Everyone knows about Diana.' Even the Ambassador from Mongolia indicated to me one day in passing he'd been keeping up on my activities. It showed his intelligence officers were in good order."

After Diana joined the mission, her mother came and learned to meditate, too.

Diana, Poss, and I had chatted a while when our ride pulled up. "Late!" Diana said. In the car were Lola, Pat (Lola's assistant), and Newt (another Soul Rush organizer). They were all smiling and finishing up the last bites of ice-cream cones.

The Soul Rush offices were located in an old Boston residential building. The sidewalk outside of it was brick, and around the door and roof was worn-but-still-fancy stonework. A black metal fence enclosed a tiny front yard which was full of ivy and had a full-leafed chestnut tree that had grown up as high as the third floor window; it stretched out, shading the street. Lola, Pat, Newt, and I would all live as well as work here. Bringing in my bags, I found comfortable quarters under the printing press.

Our office space, which took up the entire floor, was not only our temporary headquarters, it was also the permanent office of the local Boston DLM chapter and the permanent home of a number of members. It was rather small.

In the six weeks I worked there, I got to know the space very well. Around the office there were stacks of leaflets, telephones, typewriters, and telex machines at every turn. Walking through the office end to end, in one room you might find an intent audience listening to precise instructions about some project they were about to embark on. Next to them, people would be industriously typing, folding, and addressing letters. There'd be a young man speaking sincerely into the telephone, trying to calm some disturbed member of the flock: "I don't know, man, it's hard to understand why people are the way they are, but you must meditate, find that peaceful place inside . . ." In another room, there might be another group returning tired, giving each other back-rubs. In the kitchen, way in the back, several people were chopping vegetables for the evening meal. Spiritual discussions were, of course, going on everywhere, in varying degrees of intellectual depth.

Gradually our Soul Rush plans translated into hotel accommodations, parade permits, and auditorium bookings. There were eight cities, including Boston and Houston, on our final itinerary. Our route went from Boston to Plymouth Rock (on the list largely for its symbolic value), then south to Philadelphia, where we got a permit to meet at Independence Place. In Washington we were going to have a candlelight procession around the White House and a free concert the next day at the Washington Monument. After D.C. we turned to the west: to Columbus, Ohio; then south again through Indianapolis; Kansas City, Missouri; and finally Houston.

We planned to stay two or three days in each city. The first day after we arrived, the Soul Rush 500 were going to pass out leaflets and participate in media events our advance people had set up to promote the tour. On the second day in a city, we would carry out our "basic blitz": parade in the morning through the downtown area, musical one-act play in the afternoon in a downtown park, and then a free concert with Blue Aquarius in a large auditorium in the evening.

Because of the lack of time, most of our coordinating efforts were done on the phone. People called up at all hours. I took to sleeping with the phone turned way down and next to my ear, so that I could answer it within a split second of a *brring* and avoid waking up everybody else in the house. I enjoyed the early morning callers; sometimes they had interesting news from some distant outpost of the movement, and sometimes they were just lonely. BB called up on his own birthday, so I got everyone up and we sang "Happy Birthday" to him over our conference phone and then told him to go to bed.

As the date of the tour drew closer, the main thing the premie volunteers did was put up posters and give out leaflets all over the city. One hundred and fifty, sometimes two hundred people were out every night with buckets of wheatpaste and posters, creating billboards in every available space.

One night while I was leafleting in East Boston, I met Louise Day Hicks, the anti-bussing advocate, hurrying down the street. "Listen, kid," she told me, looking over the leaflet I had just handed her, "this event you are having is in the center of the city. We never go there. *This* is our home," she concluded, stamping her foot on the terra firma of East Boston. As she walked away I experienced a moment of doubt. Our gentle meditation plan seemed rather small and powerless in the face of the strong views Ms. Hicks represented.

At our public programs and on the street we tried to concentrate on telling people the value of meditation and Guru Maharaj Ji through our own experiences with them. Even though subjects like inner peace and communion with the infinite are pretty intimate stuff to talk about on Copley Square, I thought this was a fair way to go about proselytizing. For instance, if I say meditation means a lot to me and you try it and it doesn't mean much to you, fine. I haven't cheated you or led you on through false claims. We're different, that's all.

But as good as this approach sounds, in practice it is very frustrating. After months of telling people about the profound experience I was gaining through meditation and then having them stand back and smile like pleasant parents and reply, "How nice for you, as long as you are happy . . ." I began to see that this approach was like saying, "I get a thrill out of bowling." It really doesn't do that much except explain why you are down at the alley every weekend.

Because of this frustration most premies started to develop

a more flashy variety of witnessing to communicate their message. People would go out of our office with a stack of "Who is Guru Maharaj Ji?" leaflets and discreetly tell everyone who would pause long enough to hear that this Guru Maharaj Ji, age fifteen, was another Jesus Christ Here In The Flesh To Save The World. While this type of promotion appears to be a frontal attack on fixed beliefs, it did attract many people.

Justine, a top model, beauty consultant, and friend of the late Charles Revson, told me of the time when she first saw a DLM poster, circa 1972, which blatantly declared, "The Lord is Here." "That's someone who can help me," Justine thought, and wrote down the number. She is still associated with DLM today.

In addition to our on-the-street promotion of Soul Rush, we decided to have fund-raising events to promote Millennium among the premies. At one of these I was speaking, giving a typical *satsang* rap. (If you have traveled around in spiritual groups, you have probably heard this analogy many times to explain the existence of a hierarchy in the organization.)

"Divine Light Mission is like a body," I began. "And in a body all the elements must work together. The mouth eats, but every part of the body benefits. It is the job of the eyes to see and of the feet to walk, but none is greater and none is lesser. In the same way, in Divine Light Mission each person has a role. Some of us are the hands and some of us are the eyes . . ."

At this moment I was interrupted by a heckler. "And some of us are the asshole," he yelled from the back, referring to me. Immediately I appreciated this remark. Wherever I find an anarchist, I feel at home.

The night before Soul Rush was ready to roll, I went down to the bus depot and watched our painters do up the buses in the exquisite rainbow colors we had chosen. Standing next to Lola, I realized that we were halfway home. Our tiny organizing crew with the average age of 20.7 had done it. We'd raised the money, got the people, and the next morning we'd be ready to go.

Of course, there was no resting that night. The faithful wheat-paste crew, whose posters had attracted 8,000-plus to see Maharaj Ji at a program he gave in Boston, was out at work. Pat was making the final scheduling decisions. I was compiling this information into a Soul Rush manual. "Betty Boop," a friend of ours, was typing the manual on a stencil and Newt, stripped down to his undershirt, was working as a relief printer, helping the other printer who'd been working at the press sixteen hours straight. As soon as the ink was dry, people from the theater company were collating them into books, and a couple of sweethearts were binding them up. Imagine all of this happening in a 1,200-square-foot space on a warm autumn night.

The next day the "pilgrims" (our name for the Soul Rush tour personnel) started to arrive, lining up at the hotel to be checked in. They looked beautiful standing together waiting to get a hug with their orientation packets and room assignments. On the tour itself, I spent most of my time with the troops. While the other organizers were often busy with "more important things" like going out to lunch, I was left to direct the Soul Rush 500 through their day. When lines got long at mealtimes, I began a chain of stand-up back-rubbing—until eventually the whole hundreds-of-people line was transformed into a caterpillar of care in motion as each premie rubbed the back of the person in front of him. If the buses were late, I led group singing. When luggage was lost, I crawled into the luggage-carrying bellies of the buses . . .

As Susan Gregory had predicted, I was also in charge of laundry. I taught my simple, infallible, never-lose-a-sock method of laundry to a crew of fifty, and together we did the wash all night. Standing on top of a washing machine, I made my debut as a comic, telling wacky stories from my childhood.

Once, during a parade, while I was passing out issues of the newspaper I had written, a woman, astonished by the colorful good spirits of the marchers, opened her wallet and handed me all the money she had, twenty or thirty dollars. "If this is what I see on these kids' faces," she said, "I want it." A true contact high.

A number of reporters were assigned to cover Soul Rush. One of them was a seemingly charming young woman named Marilyn Webb. I was particularly fond of her because she was doing an article for my hometown paper, New York's *Village Voice*. Another group of reporters was a video crew. It seemed that every time something weird would happen, or some premie would make a dumb, fanatical, or ill-considered remark—flash—on would go the TV lights and they would start filming.

When the Soul Rush caravan rolled into Houston it was the middle of the night. We were all exhausted. The Soul Rush premies were supposed to get hotel accommodations, but I was astonished to find that they had been assigned to the "Peace Plant," an ancient Coca-Cola bottling plant which had been slightly renovated to house some of the festival staff. With this miserable omen, I went to bed with the other Soul Rushers on the floor of the "Peace Plant."

In the morning I went to the Dome for the beginning of the festival. As I expected, there were not 400,000 people there. There were plenty of premies, about 20,000, but even this number, impressive in an open field, seemed small in the vastness of the Astrodome.

In general the festival was a bore. I enjoyed seeing all of the friends I had met in other parts of the DLM community, but from a theatrical point of view, I was disappointed. Maharaj Ji's remarks were undistinguished, and I noticed his words were slurred. There were a few light notes, though, in the three days. As a joke on BB, someone tacked up a sign that said "Mars" around an empty section of seats, parroting the signs premies of France, Sweden, India, Spain, etc., had put up to announce their country of origin.

The high point of the event for me was some beers I had with Lola and the *Village Voice* reporter, Marilyn Webb. As I sat and sipped, the two of them ranted about what a disappointment the Millennium event had turned out to be. (As I discovered later, we were not the only ones for whom some alcohol was the festival's high point. Bob Mishler told me Maharaj Ji got "sloshed.")

CHAPTER

14

"WHAT A BOMB," WAS THE FIRST THING I THOUGHT ON THE morning after the program was over, as I woke up in the dilapidated old Coca-Cola plant. "What the hell am I doing here?" I rubbed my tired face and took a deep breath.

Even though I understood the complex circumstances which had made the festival into such a failure, I couldn't help but feel disappointed. It was not only a failure because few people enjoyed the three-day program. That would be tolerable, an unfortunate occurrence on par with a play bombing in the bush leagues—the theater company can always practice more and make a comeback with a better script.

But Millennium was a media event. We had promoted it actively. Journalists from all over the country were in attendance to hear what Rennie had promised would be a "practical plan for world peace." Instead of any new thoughts on a workable plan for a better world, these visiting media people found a confused jumble of inarticulately expressed ideas. The clearest remarks were the most outrageous, the Millennium Fever victims' exhortations. And, as I noticed on Soul Rush, anytime the premies started to sound dumb or crazy, on went the TV lights, to the pad went the pencils. No journalist could either resist or make sense of this odd story of foolish utopians whose leader appeared to be nothing more than a fat Indian kid in a Rolls.

"And didn't he have an ulcer?" was one reporter's last question to me at the end of the third evening.

One news story caused me great personal embarrassment. It was written by the woman from the *Village Voice* who had seemed so sweet on Soul Rush. The things I had told her, hoping to explain how fanaticism and genuine spirituality coexisted in our movement, were misquoted. Other remarks, which I had made jokingly and in high spirits, she presented as my serious beliefs.

"Do you know what came across the telex today?" Sophia, an intense 17-year-old Guru Maharaj Ji devotee (premie) asked me excitedly. "This is very confidential, but there are two beings from another planet staying at the Rainbow Inn in Houston. That's where all the premies live down there."

Soul Rush had begun, and we were on our way to Houston, where Maharaj Ji promised to present his plan for world peace. By this time I'd begun to love the premies—their energy, their enthusiasm, the way they treated each other.

"How do you know they're other beings?" I asked, hopeful that maybe it wasn't as weird as it sounded. I was thumbing through the *Boston Globe* and stopped at the page with a photograph of UFOs over Columbus, Ohio.

"Look!" Sophia jumped around me and grabbed the paper. "See, they're following Soulrush. They're going to Millennium to see Maharaj Ji 'cause he's their Lord too. He's Lord of the Universe. Really."

"Hey, Sophia, what do these beings look like?" I asked. "Has anyone actually seen them?"

"Oh, yes," she said. "They're twelve feet tall and have these big round gleaming eyes like half-dollars and fingers kind of like claws. I also heard that a big mother craft stopped above the Rainbow Inn, and a lot of baby craft went outdoors in the bottom. It was pulsating all different color lights.

"Your mind's really gonna be blown," she told me, giggling. "Bal Bhagwan Ji said that a lot of strange things are gonna happen in Houston. All of those UFOs people've been seeing are around the Gulf Coast waiting for Millennium. Maharaj Ji says he wants *all* his premies inside the Astrodome on Saturday night."

In Houston Maharaj Ji was not only going to announce the founding of an international organization to feed and shelter the world's hungry, he was not only going to initiate the building of a divine city, he was going to show the world that the Lord is indeed on this planet. By what proof we didn't know, but the UFOs were a good bet for Sophia and Tracy.

The article went on and on as if she were being paid by the word, no matter how trivial or inaccurate, obscuring and misrepresenting my actions and beliefs. I consider it libelous, and worse, it shows a lack of sense of humor. This was only one of many hundreds of such articles about the festival.

As if ruining DLM's public image were not enough, the festival also had the effect of putting the organization into a debt I estimated to be half a million dollars. (I found out later that the debt was a hundred thousand dollars more than this original estimate. In total we spent one million dollars on the Houston effort.) We owed this money to firms all over the country. The small profit that Soul Rush had made due to Lola's good sense on money matters was quickly consumed to pay a tiny portion of this large debt.

The whole thing made me feel stupid. Not stupid to be in DLM. My experiences in the early spring had given me profound reasons for joining it. In DLM I had already met many fine people who, more than any other group, shared my world view and hopes. The reason I felt stupid was because I had not done more to keep the festival from turning out as it did. Since it is always easy to think about what you could have done once something is over, on this first day after the fiasco my mind revolved around the phrases, "I could have . . ." and "If only . . ." I could have confronted BB more powerfully. If only I had been more articulate, more persuasive. . . . I could have spoken to Bob Mishler. . . . If only I had had a more clearly thought-out solution . . .

But even as my 20-20 hindsight concocted brilliant things I could have done, if only . . . , I gradually accepted that what was done was done. Working on the "today is the first day of the rest of your life" principle, I decided that I would start now and do better in the future. I would join the effort to pick up the pieces after the festival and would continue to work with the other premies to salvage what was left of DLM's public image.

To get me in the right mood for this salvaging work, I went down to the Astrohall to watch my friends on the Millennium staff take down the temporary makeshift offices they had set up there. While I was standing around leaning against a metal desk that was tipped up sideways, I was joined by Michael Donner, DLM's vice president.

When I first met Michael several months earlier I had noticed that he looked a lot like a younger version of New York's former mayor, Fiorello La Guardia, whom I knew from the statue that stands in the airport of the same name. Michael was of a muscular build, but short. When he gestured, his hands defined exact spaces and progressions. But for all of this toughness and masculine appearance, the words he said when speaking showed subtle and compassionate reasoning.

Before joining DLM, Michael had been in an anti-war group called Beaver 55 which did things like pour blood over draft files. During one of these shenanigans Michael and some of his buddies had been caught. For one charge they spent a year in a federal penitentiary; another charge was still pending. Michael might have to go back to prison. We stood together silently for a long time, and then Michael turned and spoke to me.

"You know there is a place for you in Denver, writing for the newspaper and magazine full time, if you want it." When he turned toward me I was struck by how incredibly clear his eyes were.

"I'd like to come," I replied.

* * *

Denver is a funny town. It seems to have no context for its existence, no reason for it to be there, plunked down in the middle of the desert fifty miles from the mountains. Perhaps people chose to settle there because they felt too weary to go any farther, too tired to make it over the Rockies and on to California.

For whatever reasons people settled this land a hundred years ago, I had come to Denver to be in DLM. And DLM was in Denver because Bob Mishler was there. Back in 1971 when Maharaj Ji first came to the United States, he went through Boulder, Colorado, in the late summer. Bob, a local yoga teacher, had gone to see Maharaj Ji because one of Bob's former students had given the young guru rave reviews.

When Bob learned the meditation he found he already knew the techniques. "As a matter of fact, I was teaching these same things in my yoga classes," Bob told me. But something struck him about Maharaj Ji himself. "He had both wisdom and innocence. I liked him and I wanted to help him."

Bob offered his house, down in Denver, for the traveling mahatmas to stay in when they were passing through town. Maharaj Ji must have been quite impressed with Bob, because when Bob showed him the house, Maharaj Ji asked if he could move in himself and make it DLM headquarters. From that time until late in 1976 Bob was the president of DLM and an intimate associate of Maharaj Ji.

The first night I was in Denver I stayed across the street from Bob's house; then I moved to my permanent home in one of the monastic houses a few blocks away. There were approximately thirty-five communal DLM houses in Denver, and many other single-family apartments. Many of the people who lived in my new house were also on the publications staff—my future co-workers and people I still count among my finest friends.

When I went to DLM's office building I was impressed. Headquarters occupied four floors right on Denver's main drag. The building itself had a lot of charm. Built at the turn of the century, it had sculpted stone sides and a row of arched windows at the sixth-floor level. In the middle of the modern, less decorative buildings in downtown Denver, the Kittredge Building looked like a small castle.

The building was owned by Joe Gould, an eccentric and extremely wealthy man with offices there and in Las Vegas. Joe claimed to have had his start in Chicago as "Al Capone's shoeshine boy." Maharaj Ji and Joe were good friends and were alike in many ways, both being extremely short and successful on their own terms, in their chosen businesses.

What DLM had inside Joe's building impressed me more than the building's location and architecture. There was all of the photographic, typesetting, copy camera, platemaking and printing equipment of a good-sized graphic and printing company.

After I settled into my office and the initial razzle-dazzle wore off, my mind returned to the trouble the mission faced: half a million dollars owed to businesses all over the country. Now where could I get half a million dollars? I looked out the window of my office and began to wonder. I could get a job, I thought, as I noticed clouds gathering and snow beginning to fall.

My new "service," as people in DLM like to call their organizational assignments, was in the DLM publications, covering the Family beat—the activities of Guru Maharaj Ji and his kin—for the *Divine Times*. I was also asked to write assorted feature articles of a general nature.

To help with the debt I planned to take some off-hours job which still gave me some time for my service. After a week of pounding the pavement, the only employment I could find—I didn't go to any laundries—was an assembly-line job in a Christmas wreath factory for a buck sixty an hour. Work started at seven in the morning and went on with two ten-minute breaks until two-thirty in the afternoon.

The factory was kept very cold, to avoid wilting the greens. It was staffed primarily by non-English-speaking people. In front of me on the assembly line were four or five Orientals who must have worked there for many seasons. They could whip out wreaths like crazy. Further down the line were several Spanish-speaking women who showed less interest in their productivity.

Whatever boredom I suffered at the wreath-making line was quickly compensated for by my service. All of Guru Maharaj Ji's family were in Denver, except for Maharaj Ji himself. Sensing that Millennium was the end of her and BB's reputation among the American DLM members, Mata was making a desperate effort to consolidate her power base.

One day several weeks after the festival, I went to the house DLM had bought for Maharaj Ji and his family, to attend a reception Mata was holding for the housemothers, the young women who took care of the domestic side of the headquarters staff's lives. This apparently innocent gathering was the beginning of Mata's many attempted coups.

Mata, wrapped in her familiar pink sari, was wearing her diamond nose ring. "You are not appreciated in your work," she exhorted them through a translator. (She spoke only Hindi.) "You should go out and tell people about this love, this Knowledge, this truth. . . . Anna, where would you like to go?" She pointed to a large map of the world she had set up behind her.

Naturally this created a rather uncomfortable situation at headquarters. Some housemothers, anxious to end their bondage to the stove and washing machine, took Mata up on her offer. They collected enough money for a ticket and went off to some other, hopefully more pleasant, part of the world. Others smiled sweetly at Mata, then left the meeting shaking their heads. "She's really flipped, hasn't she?" I heard Anna comment to her friend as she walked to her car.

This was a situation that Maharaj Ji would clearly have to deal with himself. Unfortunately, Maharaj Ji was out of town trying to form a new family for himself. He had met a young woman shortly before the festival and had fallen in love with her, although this was not clear until a few months later. Since it was hard to know exactly what definitive action any of us should take with Mata and her boys, people at headquarters resorted to that old social formula: be polite, talk about the weather, and smile.

But on some occasions this would not do. For example, once the mission directors were having a meeting to figure out some basic economy measures. They had already gotten rid of all but one of our WATS lines and cut back on non-essential personnel. Now they were looking for new ways to economize. Mata, who was downstairs attending a DLM program, heard about the meeting upstairs and wanted to attend.

Since I had a key to the elevator, I took her upstairs and then stood in the doorway and watched. Her remarks to the group were excessive and cruel. Some of them the translator would not repeat. At the end of fifteen minutes, several of the directors, male and female, were in tears. Holding part of the general ledger in her hand, she looked a lot like Joe McCarthy with his list of Communists.

If politeness kept some premies from insulting Mata to her face, they got back at her in other ways. A few people started imitating her high, whining voice and made slightly derogatory remarks about Indians and Indian culture. For example, there are many Indian scriptures whose names, to the American ear, sound like the names of Indian food. People would joke that we were going to have "pourris" (Indian bread) and "Puranas" (Indian scriptures) to mop up our plates after dinner.

Mata could see she was not gaining any ground. When she and BB learned that Maharaj Ji would be arriving in Denver, they must have decided to take the money and run.

This tactic, however, would not have been discovered had it not been for Freddy, one of the young men who lived in the house with me. BB was going to the airport and Freddy was taking his bags. When it came time for the plane to leave, Freddy absentmindedly left one of the attaché cases on the runway. When the airport officials opened it up to find out its owner, they discovered a suitcase full of $100 bills. *The Rocky Mountain News,* a Denver daily, ran a story under the headline, "Franklin Never Flew the Friendly Skies," which represented the detached and amused attitude the Denver citizens were beginning to take toward having the guru in their town.

But the intrigue did not end here. Mata, BB, and Bhole Ji left Denver and regrouped in New York, where BB had had some popularity in years past. You'd think his popularity would have worn a little thin because he had predicted such an adverse fate for the Big Apple and all her inhabitants, the pre-Millennium earthquakes. But instead they were welcomed and allowed to stay in the house reserved for Maharaj Ji in Westbury, Long Island. Firmly settled in, Mata and BB encouraged the local premies in their plans for a birthday party for Maharaj Ji, who would be sixteen on December tenth. Then they tried to get Maharaj Ji to come, to see them on their own turf. Maharaj Ji's new girlfriend, Marilyn, was not invited. From the start Mata had insisted, according to those who translated her Hindi for me, that Marilyn was lower class, a dirty American, not a fit match for their little Maharaj Ji.

Maharaj Ji did not want to attend the party. When conventional methods of invitation like flowers and phone calls failed to attract him, Mata and BB tried another tack. They sent a message to Maharaj Ji that Mata was on her deathbed, using a weeping premie as the courier. Maharaj Ji would have to come immediately if he wanted to see Mata before she died. Finally, at the last minute, Maharaj Ji got on a plane and went to New York. When he discovered Mata was not on her deathbed, he seemed furious, according to a friend of mine who was there. But since he was in town anyway, he decided to attend the birthday party. Several thousand people had gathered who genuinely wanted to wish him well, unaware of the part this party had played in the plot behind the scenes.

Amazingly, nothing Maharaj Ji did in public that day gave them any inkling of the troubles. Even at this late date, in the face of Mata and BB, Maharaj Ji was still holding to his stand-and-smile-with-the-family policy.

From my vantage at headquarters, I saw the real story which was hidden from the majority of premies. This private information put me in an awkward position. Since I was supposed to cover the "holy family" news for the premie paper, I thought I should write something about it. But I knew what a delicate situation existed. I did not want to jeopardize Maharaj Ji's position. If push came to shove, I knew Mata would try to use her power as Maharaj Ji's legal guardian and make him return to India, never to be heard from again. Then I would have lost my friend and guru.

After talking with Matthew Austin, the *Divine Times* editor, we decided to go ahead with some sort of series on the situation. But when Matthew proposed this idea to Bob Mishler, Bob nixed it, saying, "It would confuse the premies; besides, it is not what Maharaj Ji wants."

That it would "confuse the premies" struck Matthew and me as absurd. Matthew said he didn't want to be part of any "paternalistic cover-up," but I was willing to give Maharaj Ji some credit for his discretion. After all, he was not the first of my young associates who had trouble with his parents. In my opinion it all added up to a waiting game. Maharaj Ji was holding out for his eighteenth birthday when, by Indian law, he would be a man, free and clear of his mother's legal clutches.

In reaction to his frustration, Matthew tried to take the newspaper in a different direction. He wanted to make it more of a general interest publication with a spiritual perspective, rather than what he called a "propaganda rag."

As we worked together on the new paper idea, Matthew and I became good friends. Since we both lived in the same house, we usually walked to the office together on the mornings when I was not working in the Christmas-wreath factory. Matthew was thirty-two years old and had a good deal of writing experience. He had started out in New York as a copywriter fresh out of college; over eight years he gradually became dissatisfied with his life and his Greenwich Village apartment. From New York he moved to Boston to make a new start on a life outside the nine-to-five subway-to-subway grind. In Boston Matthew started a small spiritual newspaper called *Boston Public Gardens*. It was a fine little paper, and I remember seeing it when I lived in Maine. Matthew joined DLM in 1972 and toward the end of that year he took over *Divine Times* for the mission. Even though Matthew had, like me, adopted the ashram lifestyle, which did not allow drugs, alcohol, or cigarettes, he had never quite adjusted. Sometimes in the office he smelled of Scotch, and he kept a stash of marihuana tucked away up in the *Divine Times* office's false ceiling to enjoy late at night with some of the other people on the *DT* staff. On our morning walks downtown we sometimes stopped as many as three times over the twenty-five-block distance so that Matthew could have coffee and a cigarette on his way to work. Since I have never smoked cigarettes nor had any desire whatsoever to smoke them, the ashram restriction did not bother me.

Coincidentally, another friend on the publications staff had also been in Boston putting out another paper at the same time Matthew was there. This was Saul Bear, who lived in the same house with Tom and me and was the Assistant Editor of DLM's four-color monthly magazine. Saul's Boston paper was a monthly called *Lavender Vision*, which was aimed at a homosexual audience. Because of its coherent format and writing, *Lavender Vision* was a leading force in Boston's gay civil liberties effort at that time. When I was in Maine, I had also seen this paper, as well as Matthew's.

I thoroughly enjoyed my association with this varied group of people, many of whom had been successful in other fields before joining DLM. The office suite down the hall from me was jokingly referred to as the Harvard-Radcliffe Club, because its three inhabitants were all graduates of that venerable institution.

Leaving New York a few hours after the party was over, Maharaj Ji returned to California and his sweetheart. Raja Ji, the brother most close to Maharaj Ji in age and temperament, was also having a love affair—a fact which infuriated Mata all the more. Raja Ji's romance was with Claudia Littmann, a European model whose father was at one time chief of police in Frankfurt. One day, as I was leafing through a graphic magazine to get ideas for our new-style *Divine Times,* I saw an advertisement that Claudia had done before joining DLM. Claudia and Marilyn lived together in an apartment in Marina del Ray, California. A few days after Maharaj Ji got into L.A., Mata, BB, and Bhole Ji also arrived, making themselves at home in Maharaj Ji's small house on Sunset Boulevard.

Meanwhile, back in my life, *I* was having a less serious love affair. Although in coming to Denver I had agreed to live in a monastic way, I found it rather difficult to do so. From my short experience, there was no substitute for the deep and happy satisfaction of making love. On a few occasions during that cold winter of '73–'74, I broke my monastic commitment.

At the end of the Christmas season, I was laid off my job at the wreath factory. They did a small business throughout the year for funeral homes, but they no longer needed the extra workers they took on at Christmas. To add to my unemployment, at the same time DLM's newspaper went out of business for lack of funds. On the day that I was about to start looking for work in the local laundries, one of the DLM directors approached me with a much more attractive offer. His idea was for me to write a gourmet vegetarian cookbook with a really excellent cook who lived in New York City.

With a sigh of relief, I accepted this job and began writing up some guidelines for the book. At that time DLM was running a restaurant in midtown Manhattan that served tasty food and was called the Alive Kitchen. It seemed logical to me if I was writing the *Alive Kitchen Cookbook* and working with a New York cook, I should go to New York and see them both.

While I was waiting for a car ride east—plane fare cost too much—Maharaj Ji announced that he was going to do a tour of all the DLM branches around the country. Denver was not the only place where things were dark and the living was lean; all the premie communities were in a similar slump. Maharaj Ji wanted to make a tour and cheer up the troops. This also offered him a discreet way to get Mata out of his hair; however, she insisted on joining him in his travels. So much for that plan.

The first stop in Maharaj Ji's tour was Denver. He planned to be there for Valentine's Day. Not having much to do while I waited around for a ride, I volunteered for the "World Peace Corps" or "WPC" duty, which was a corps of sweet-looking ushers and more brawny strongarms whose job was to control the crowds at Maharaj Ji's program. Raja Ji was thought of as the "spiritual director" of the WPC. One advantage of this job was the close proximity to Maharaj Ji, himself.

Standing on the stage with Maharaj Ji or at the door of where he was staying, you could get a good look at him, hear what he really thought about things, and enjoy his relaxed personality in a way that was impossible sitting so far away in the audience of one of his large programs. From so close you might even get to understand the enigma: this little fellow from India who suffered his pains so quietly and still wanted to save the whole world.

While I was working for the World Peace Corps during Maharaj Ji's Denver programs, I had an interesting experience with a reporter from the *Denver Post*. The reporter was planning to do an article for the *Post*'s Sunday magazine. He was very open-minded about the Mission and the Knowledge, so he decided to participate in a ritual called "Darshan" which usually attracts only premies. In the Darshan ceremony, the premies line up and wait their turns to go before Maharaj Ji. The first time a person is involved in Darshan, they can ask for "holy breath," which is a special initiation which only the guru can give. Then, after a person has had "holy breath," he may go up for Darshan again anytime, though on subsequent occasions there will be no further initiation. The person may offer a flower to Maharaj Ji, kiss his feet, or just give him a good look in the eye, whatever suits.

This reporter got in the line, taking a daffodil. He bowed and placed the flower at Maharaj Ji's feet. When he stood up, he told me he felt a rush of ecstasy. He stumbled away, almost falling. I reached over and caught him, since I was standing next to Maharaj Ji's chair. He was laughing and crying at once. I helped him to a bench nearby. "I couldn't see. There was too much golden light," he exclaimed.

Later Michael Donner related this incident to Maharaj Ji and I corroborated it. Maharaj Ji turned away nonchalantly and replied, "Oh, that guy, he's just eaten too many chili peppers." When the reporter heard this remark, he was astounded. Chili peppers were one of his favorite foods. This reporter wrote a lovely piece about the young guru.

After Maharaj Ji left Denver, I got a ride to New York. I stayed there several weeks and then returned to Denver with the cook-collaborator. While I was working on the book proposal, tasting good food and writing little stories about the ingredients, I continued my involvement with the World Peace Corps. The person in charge of the national WPC had been nicknamed "Lemon" by Maharaj Ji because of his seemingly sour disposition. Raja Ji and Lemon were good friends. I found Lemon to be quite a good companion on some occasions. Now that the Mission had so little work to do because of its financial troubles, Lemon thought it was an ideal time to reevaluate the Mission's focus. "Action's where it's at; not all this talk," he insisted over and over. Lemon thought the organization would be better off as a social service group. "World *Peace* Corps, man. World Peace *Corps.* That means work." He shouted and pounded on his desk. Lemon had a slightly military quality which he enhanced by wearing dark suits and always keeping the corners of his mouth firmly in a frown. As a sidekick he had a smart aide named Gordon Petty, who could articulate in less passionate tones what Lemon was thinking. Gordon always spoke softly, almost in a monotone, which contrasted strongly with Lemon's more emotional cadence.

"We should organize the premies into meaningful community action groups," Gordon said, explaining Lemon's thoughts. "This will foster discipline and compassion. It will also help the premies become more rooted in practical values. Through firsthand experience of real suffering they will understand how much work is needed in the world and how crucial it is for us to begin. Beyond even this, volunteering will not hinder the financial recovery of DLM. It is a perfect time to start this work."

Since I was a "writer," Lemon asked me if I would write up some proposals for him. Since I agreed with Gordon and his idea of how DLM should be run, I took the job. Though they were a comical pair to be aligned with, I liked their thinking. Lola, whom I knew from Soul Rush, did too, and soon she moved into the house where Lemon organized his projects.

This house was located in the all-black section of Denver, far outside the traditional premie neighborhood. Lemon had chosen this out-of-the-way location to emphasize his distaste for the administration which had put together Millennium. Even before the festival Lemon had felt a definite antagonism toward DLM programs. He thought many of them were hot air and he made sure everyone knew how he felt.

After I finished the cookbook proposal, I was out of a job again. I did not plan to write the cookbook if a major publisher was not going to buy it. I knew we did not have the expertise to distribute it ourselves, even if we did have the facilities to print it. Rather than go back to the director who had gotten me started on the cookbook and ask for a new assignment, I decided to help Lemon in the WPC. While tactfully assuring my friends in the leadership of DLM that I was not writing them off by joining this slightly renegade operation, I packed my bags and moved to the WPC house, becoming one more among the white folks on the block.

Analyzing the outfit, I saw that WPC had the same problem that Good Day Market had faced in Maine: the volunteers needed a source of money so that they could keep body and soul together while they did their good deeds around the community. The answer seemed the same: start a service company. Nobody liked the name Denver-America Contracting, so we settled on something more "spiritual": Rainbow Community Services. We had cards printed up and were in business. On our best day we employed thirty people.

Living in the WPC house, I had access to a lot of information that would not normally come my way even on the *Divine Times* staff. For instance, Raja Ji, Guru Maharaj Ji's still-faithful brother, told me how he had secretly married Claudia while Mata was away on tour with Maharaj Ji. Then when Mata returned from touring, Raja Ji said, he no longer felt able to keep up the charade and went to face his mother with his new wife. Raja Ji said Mata was livid with rage and would not allow him and Claudia to come inside Maharaj Ji's L.A. residence. Instead, she ordered the mahatmas who were present to go outside and beat up Raja Ji and Claudia while they stood in the driveway on Sunset Boulevard.

When Maharaj Ji returned and saw his brother black-and-blue and his brother's wife with a bloody face, he became extremely frightened, according to Bob Mishler. He called Bob on the telephone and finally took a strong stand in regard to his family. Bob remembered the conversation this way: "Maharaj Ji was extremely upset. He told me 'Get them out of the country. Deport them, anything. Anything. I don't care what you do. Just get them out of here.' " Bob was glad to do it. "I'd had enough of their tricks." So using what Bob described as a "variety of intimidation tactics," he convinced them to go back to India. While Mata and BB were preparing to leave, Raja Ji came to stay with us in Soultown and Maharaj Ji sought refuge in the Denver residence reserved for him. Maharaj Ji refused to see Mata or BB before they left. Several times I remember Lemon driving to the airport in the middle of the night to dissuade BB from going to see Maharaj Ji at his home in Denver.

"Finally," Bob said, "I arranged for Bal Bhagwan Ji to speak to Maharaj Ji on the phone. Maharaj Ji told Bal Bhagwan Ji that if he would go back to India and take Mata, then he, Maharaj Ji, would return to India himself on May 24."

On May 24, 1974, Maharaj Ji and Marilyn were married in a small chapel in the foothills of the Rockies. The next day the news appeared all over the world. For most premies, this was a very happy day, but for Mata and BB, Maharaj Ji had committed an act of war. Sitting in India, they planned a full-scale campaign against their youngest kin.

I could see that Raja was not taking it well. With the lines so clearly drawn he began expanding his existing fascination for guns and violence. Like Maharaj Ji, Raja Ji had started to drink. Though I love to drink from time to time, I never do so before the end of the afternoon. Raja Ji sometimes started much earlier than that. One evening I sat with him and Claudia as they drank. Slowly the conversation turned from an interesting discussion to a series of slurred comments about where do the bubbles come from in champagne. This is spirituality? I thought to myself. This sort of incident and the seemingly endless difficulties Guru Maharaj Ji had with his family were wearing me out.

I started to wonder if maybe the Mission was destined to fail; if from the beginning the odds had been stacked too heavily against Maharaj Ji. Even though Knowledge was an excellent product, probably the best on the market, the mismanagement of the business and the ineptitude of the sales force might be too great to overcome.

This idea depressed me. It made me sick to think all the effort I had made and all the efforts my sincere friends had made would come to nothing. I didn't like the idea that people who might have benefitted from meditation would never hear about Knowledge because our Guru's life was so flashy, his family so greedy.

I thought of the Christian Church and the profound realizations of its early members and then I thought about the Church today and how little spiritual progress seemed to be happening in it. Full of these weary thoughts, I went to the office building to see Saul Bear, who had moved out of the ashram after the magazine folded. He was in a joyous mood and grabbed me to dance while he hummed some music. I couldn't help but smile.

"The paper's going back in print," he said. "Somebody donated $350,000. Come on kid, cheer up. Let's go out dancing tonight."

That sounded like a good idea. Knowing the debt was reduced to a manageable and payable level lifted a weight off my back. In a peculiar way it signaled to me that my responsibility to the Mission was over. The commitment I had made when joining the Millennium staff was complete. When I met Saul that night I was in a fine humor and stayed out until three in the morning. When I got up the next day I knew what I should do. The time had come for Sophia to take a vacation. And let me assure you, after a year of poverty, chastity, and obedience, I was ready to make money, make love, and make decisions.

CHAPTER

15

I STOOD AT THE DOOR AND GAZED ACROSS THE POOL. HUMID air was not common in Denver. Even humid air with a tinge of chlorine was a welcome change. "I'll take it," I said to the renting agent who was winding up my tour of the building. Now that I was going on vacation I planned to do it up right. This building had all the luxuries. It was managed for young people, singles with money. The pool into whose blue waters I was now gazing was not the only pool around, either: there was also a whirlpool and a pool table—and a sauna bath, next to the steam bath, down the hall from the game room.

My apartment was upstairs—push nine in the elevator and there you were. The terrace looked north, and since the ninth story is above the usual height of houses in Denver, I could see clearly for miles and miles, all the way out to where Denver ended and became fields for grain and, farther than that, open range. With a good spyglass I could have spotted the cattle grazing. In the early morning I could see the sun come up and in the evening I could see it set over the Rockies in the west. Once the sun was gone and the city lights came on, I looked out across a deep blue field filled with points of light. In my imagination they were stars. On my terrace I was surfing in the sky.

Once I settled in, I began to invite friends over to visit. Several times a week I would entertain, take my friends for a sauna and swim, give them a drink and dinner, laugh over coffee until past midnight. Some nights I went out dancing, down to the local disco with six or seven pals. In the morning I slept until nine or ten and then meditated in a leisurely way. After that I would read, write letters to old friends, do whatever came into my mind. For cash, to support my stay-at-home vacation, I worked a few days a week. It was easy to find work with one of my old partners from the Rainbow Services. We planted flowers in people's yards for six dollars an hour. With no car, no mortgage, no children, no life insurance, no college loan, I didn't need too many hours of this work to keep me in high style.

After about a month of this decadent life, I felt satisfied, fully rested and refreshed from my year-and-a-half as a work-frenzied monk in a guru cult. Come September 1974, I felt it was time to take stock of my position and figure out where to go from here.

In trying to decide what to do next, I played a game of imagination with myself. I imagined myself in all sorts of positions and situations to find out which one I would enjoy the most and find satisfying. First I ran through all the conventional models: I imagined myself as rich and famous, a top businesswoman, the lady in the limousine. "Home, James!" I said, pulling the blinds of my long blue Fleetwood Westport. Then I tried on (trumpets, please) the Young Doctor. I pictured myself staring sincerely into the eyes of a patient while I held his hand, commenting wisely on his condition. Next, I became President of the United States— —reporters everywhere, aides coming running in and out with weighty bills for my signature or veto. A bevy of nice-looking young men are waiting in the wings for my affections.

No, none of these seemed quite right. How about a successful artist: There I am on the cover of *Time* proclaiming "The Joy of Art" and watching my work—in many media— acclaimed as opening new, startling frontiers in beauty and human imagination. In publications ranging from *Art News* to the SoHo paper my name is known. That sounds pretty good, I thought, but *Time* magazine?

Amid all this whimsy, I did manage some serious thinking. The conclusion I reached about my immediate future—leaving these other fantasies for a later time—was that I wanted to go back and give Divine Light Mission another go. One of the main things that made up my mind was a visit I had made to the headquarters a few weeks before. Walking around the offices, I found many of the same people were there as when I left, but the focus of their work had changed considerably.

Back in April 1973, before all the Mission's activities and plans were supplanted by the Millennium festival production, Guru Maharaj Ji had made a film about his vision for DLM. In it he proposed a new organization, to be called Divine United Organization, and outlined its humanitarian goals. DUO—the name is pronounced rather than the letters spelled out—would work in many areas: health care, education, food co-ops, the arts, as well as the traditional social service areas of emergency relief and visiting the sick and institutionalized. When the idea originally was put forth, premie enthusiasm rallied around it. A clip was attached to Maharaj Ji's original film wherein Bob Mishler suggested that DUO could also be a method by which premies could be employed. Businesses could be organized which were ecologically sound and spiritually elevating for both patron and employee.

Now, at headquarters, the energy of the one-hundred-person staff went into the development of the different branches of DUO. Mark Retzloff, a friend of mine from the Houston food service, was planning to link up the thirty-five DLM food co-ops and four retail food stores premies were running around the country and make them into one "Rainbow Grocery" chain. Natural food was Mark's main interest. Prior to working in DLM he had been the largest distributor of natu-

ral foods in Michigan. Now he was trying to "foster cooperation based on spiritual unity, rather than the profit motive."

Another person I knew from Houston was pulling together the premies in the performing arts to see if the many
premie musical groups that already existed could help each
other by sharing equipment, ideas, and contacts. DLM's
dance troupe was planning a national tour. The Soul Rush
theater group was at work on some new material.

Social service was an area of special importance in DUO.
Rennie Davis, now recovered from the festival, was working
on an idea called "Day of Thanks," a Thanksgiving Day
effort to involve several thousand premies across the country
in hospital visitation programs. "Then," Susan Gregory said,
"once the premies realize what a joyful experience it is to
do this kind of service for others, they'll want to sign up
for many more DUO social service programs."

Looking around, I could see that DLM had thoroughly
recovered from last year's festival bummer. Things were in
bloom. For a change, DLM seemed going in the right direction. When I saw Saul, he told me that after the magazine went back in print he had been promoted to full editor.
"You want a job?" he asked me. "I could use a writer. You
could write children's stories, or better yet, do the 'There
is a Knowledge . . .' series."

"There is a Knowledge . . ." was a part of the magazine
Saul used to write before he was editor. It explained in
practical terms the benefits of meditation through examples
of premies' lives and experiences.

"They're into it now. What a change," he said, describing
the new thrust in DLM's outreach programs: to talk about
meditation, rather than resort to the "flashy witnessing" style
I saw during Soul Rush.

At the time when Saul asked me to come back on the staff,
I did not take the offer too seriously. I was still on vacation,
I told him. But now, with the demand for flower gardeners
on the wane, I was looking around for new employment.

When I spoke to the local director about moving back in, he was hesitant at first. He wasn't admitting anyone into the ashram at that time. So I called up my friend Michael Donner, who was now U.S. national director, and told him the situation. An old-style radical, Michael had no taste for bureaucracy. He phoned the local director and asked what was up. "No problem here," the local man said. I moved back into DLM and after a month I was once more working on the Mission's newspaper, *Divine Times*.

A few things had changed at the paper. My old boss, Matthew Austin, had retired, as editor and as premie. He had married a woman fifteen years older than he and become an instant father to an eighteen-year-old young woman. From time to time, Matthew invited me over for a glass of wine or I ran into him on the street. But he wasn't interested in the organization anymore. He didn't even want to talk about it.

Now another person was giving the *Divine Times* editor post a try. This was Dan Hinckley, who until this time had always lingered on the periphery of the publications circle sporting the catchall title of "Research Director." Dan was a very interesting young man, and as I worked with him, he as editor and I as assistant editor—not assistant *to* the editor, mind you—we became very close and loving in a platonic way, like brother and sister.

Again I benefitted from the one advantage of the ashram's chastity vow: it allowed a person to develop strong relationships with persons of the opposite sex without a jumble of complications. I have heard that some people see every other person as a potential bedmate. I, however, have never felt this way. If I like someone I want to become more intimate, but this does not always mean sex. I remember several occasions at parties when I'd been talking with a man and suddenly the mood changed. "Let's go to bed," he would suggest, usually in a more subtle way. If I was not interested that was the end of the conversation. Period.

Since Dan and I had both made monastic vows we did not have to wonder whether or not our closeness suggested we should have sex. I appreciated many things about Dan. I liked how big he was. I am five foot ten, and he was several inches over six feet. Where I couldn't reach up on a high shelf, he had no trouble. He was quite strong and built *big*, like a bear. To add to this bear-like quality, Dan's mother lived in Hickory Corners, Michigan. From time to time Dan played the flute and wrote poetry, but neither as a virtuoso.

With ease, Dan could quote Maslow, Einstein, Toynbee, Kant, and other big names. But he was no effete intellectual. If something broke, he opened his files and in the back of the stacks, behind the folders full of weighty thoughts, was a full tool kit. The hammer in it was a clue to Dan's nature. It was a twenty-ounce—the heavy kind framers use to drive nails into two-by-fours when they are putting up houses. With no rough work like this to do, Dan used the hefty tool delicately, putting in a tack or giving something the tiniest tap to set it right in place.

As assistant editor, my responsibility was national news, reporting on the diverse activities of premies in the United States. All around the country people in DLM communities were very busy with new projects. Many of them had begun small businesses ranging from a pottery shop in Florida and a woodworking studio in Georgia to a theater coffee shop in San Francisco and a laundromat/dry cleaner's in Denver. People were beginning to come to introductory programs which had been restructured to present Knowledge in a more intelligible way.

Many premies were getting married, settling down, and buying homes. Maharaj Ji and Marilyn were expecting a baby. They even had gotten themselves a new nest in Malibu, California. While looking for news of the L.A. area, I heard several stories about Maharaj Ji from one of the people who lived in Malibu with him.

When Guru Maharaj Ji moved into his new house, he immediately began to improve his property through some rather extensive landscaping projects. Since he loves machines, Maharaj Ji decided to buy a tractor which he would sometimes drive around the canyons where he lived. One day as Maharaj Ji was rounding a bend, he came to a place where a large luxury car was hanging perilously over the edge of the road. The despondent driver was sitting on the ground in a well-tailored suit with his head in his hands.

Without saying a word, Maharaj Ji stopped and jumped off the tractor. He whipped out a set of chains, attached them to the bumper, and pulled the car back on the road. By the time the driver stood up to see what was going on, Maharaj Ji had already packed up his chains, jumped on the tractor, and was heading off, full throttle down the canyon.

"Oh, then he's in good spirits," I inquired of this correspondent. Maharaj Ji had seemed very happy when I had seen him during a business trip he had made to Denver a month before; but since I remembered how he had hidden his feelings about his family, it was hard for me to know his true mood.

"Sure, ever since Mata Ji left he's been very happy. I'd say he's back to his old merry pranksterish self again," my source said, and then related this story:

Maharaj Ji had bought a book at a novelty store which to all external appearances was a hardcover called *Sex Handbook;* but when you opened it, you received an electric shock. He spent several days "souping up" the wiring so that it would give a more powerful shock, and then one day when his brother, Raja Ji, came to visit him at his Malibu estate, he thought he'd try it out. In the car with him Raja Ji had brought several other people, including his wife, Claudia.

"Raja Ji! Raja Ji!" Maharaj Ji ran up to the car to greet him with the book in his hand. The others were still in the car as Maharaj Ji said to Raja Ji, with a tone of deep tenderness, "Look what Marilyn has just given me," pressing the book into Raja Ji's hands.

"Oh," said Raja Ji with much interest, and then, *"Ahhhh!"* when he opened the book. Just then Claudia came up. "Oh, Claudia! Look what Marilyn has just given me," he said to Claudia with the same tender tone.

"Oh," she said, and then, *"Ahhhh!"*

Each of the next three people arrived and they in turn fell for the trick. Then when there were no more, Maharaj Ji took the book back and walked into the house, satisfied that he had shocked enough people with his *Sex Handbook*.

My new office was still down the hall from the Harvard-Radcliffe Club, whose members continued to produce articles and ideas. I shared the office with Saul, who now wanted to move back into the ashram too.

Saul edited Guru Maharaj Ji's lectures for publication. When a particular transcript showed Guru Maharaj Ji's philosophical remarks "waxing incoherent," as Saul said, he would simply throw up his hands in the air and cheerfully, mischievously, declare, "Oh, he didn't mean *that*." Then, licking his fine editing pencil, he would squint his eyes and write in something that sounded a little better.

Saul's authority as an editor in DLM went back a long way. He had put out the first national DLM newsletter, writing it and then cranking it out himself on a mimeograph machine in Bob Mishler's basement in 1971. Now, as editor of a monthly four-color slick, Saul, more than almost anybody else in DLM, could testify to the organization's progress.

CHAPTER

16

ONE DAY AS SAUL AND I WERE GOING DOWN TO GET SOME TEA in the cafeteria, we found ourselves in the middle of a meeting which was being held there. Tiptoeing over to the hot water dispenser, we picked out some blends—Mellow Mint for me and Sleepy Time for Saul. While the tea was steeping, we perked up our ears, trying to eavesdrop inconspicuously. The subject of this meeting seemed to be some sort of big deal reorganization plan. This was nothing new in itself. From my observation, the main function of high level administrators seemed to be moving offices and changing titles. But there was something peculiar about the way these people were talking. It took a while to place it, but then it came to me. They were all speaking in the passive voice. The problems of the organization "were being analyzed, prioritized, and finalized," but by whom it wasn't clear. "Debts had been incurred," but nobody seemed to know who spent the money. "Time lines were going to be created," and then "they were going to be met," all by equally shadowy, unmentioned hands.

"Good Lord," Saul quipped. "There is nobody here."

Walking upstairs with my Mellow Mint, I wondered if at a certain point in a company's development some great *deus ex machina* suddenly grabs hold of the corporation, disembodies it, and starts to operate it independent of any person's talking, typing, or planning.

Over the next few weeks I continued thinking along these lines, believing that perhaps this point had arrived for DLM. One of the main things contributing to this impression was the arrival of Michael Dettmers, a former junior executive in one of the larger American multinationals. His ideas were all management-textbook stuff: organizational charts and management-by-objectives. He came to Denver to set up some systems for managing our money, but when he arrived he got to work on other areas. His first project was redoing the organizational chart. After the juggling of boxes and lines was done, Michael was a vice president and we, the artists' and writers' group, were called Research and Development.

Michael believed in "professional managers." He thought a person's experience and familiarity with an area of work were not as important as their proven abilities as a manager. The criteria of the manager's ability? "Why, how well he executes the objectives of the organization," Michael explained. And who sets the objectives? "The top management, of course." Undoubtedly, this hierarchical structure and its performance evaluation scheme comprise a perfectly fine battle plan for making money in a multinational. But as I considered Michael's ideas, I had a vague bad feeling. I didn't know exactly why, but I felt fairly sure his were not the best guidelines for running an organization whose goal is to raise consciousness.

But, for better or for worse, Michael was there and he was in charge. Because of his belief in "professional managers," R&D soon had one, in the person of Jeff Grossberg, who arrived in December. By January the word "executive" was popping up more often and more seriously. Although DLM had always had a certain corporate pretense—I think it is something Ma Bell installed with the first WATS line—it was not something the people in the DLM general membership paid much attention to. My impression was that most premies just assumed that a few business-like formalities were necessary for the legal and financial stability of our movement. In a leader, however, most DLM members were not looking for a guy in a three-piece suit, sitting behind a nine-foot teak desk and with an impressive résumé. Instead they wanted someone with awareness and an ability to communicate his or her insights. For this reason a heavy-duty title did not command instant respect from the membership. In fact, a title often had the opposite effect. Since the people whom the title was supposed to impress were largely unmoved, it was difficult for the managers to get swelled heads about their positions.

But, believe me, they tried. In early 1973 the "executive group" rented a place to live which they named the "Executive House." This move caused such scorn and ridicule that the house was dissolved several months later. The things which enhance power in an ordinary hierarchy diminished it in ours. If a person seemed to be a real mover, an aggressive go-getter within DLM, this was often taken as a sign that this individual did not have what it took to be a leader. Premies were looking for inspirational examples of selflessness, not someone who would help them become rich.

The man who preceded Michael Dettmers as financial director was a good example of a popular DLM figure. Although he handled DLM's three-and-a-half-million-dollar budget from 1972 to the middle of 1974, when he retired, he was most widely recognized for his lighthearted approach to the heavenly life. His philosophy was that there was no reason for guilt or fear; that God-realization was beautiful, profound, and even fun. His public talks, even at fundraising events, were sprinkled with such corny one-liners as, "My housemother has so little culture she can't even make yogurt." And, "Do you meditate on an empty stomach? No, I prefer a pillow myself."

Michael Dettmers, on the other hand, never made a joke. I heard him say he felt it "unfitting to the corporate image." Instead, at a staff meeting, he did things like explain the new organizational chart while his secretary indicated the chain of command with a pointer. He never had to explain the first three rows. They were in large type, plain as day, and everybody could see they looked like this:

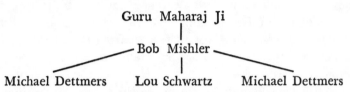

Now that Michael Dettmers was affirming the importance of the executive, the people who had an interest in things like organizational titles and status found they had some support. I am not suggesting here that Michael Dettmers himself was a power-hungry status-seeker; I am just saying that Michael's emphasis on the importance of hierarchy, authority, and chain of command gave the small group of people with titles a chance to have the sense of authority they missed in their previous bids for status.

What all this boiled down to in terms of Research and Development's new "professional manager," Jeff Grossberg, was that immediately after arriving Jeff claimed the best desk for himself. He took the tape player we kept to listen to rough copies of the radio tapes DLM made. And Jeff eyed with desire the small office refrigerator which all of us had used to store our snacks. Pacing around our offices, Jeff appeared to be delighted. He was finally getting some status.

Aware of Jeff's lusting for the little fridge, we decided to steal it before he installed it in his own office. We knew, through our network of interorganizational contacts (primarily secretaries) that Mac, the supply clerk, was going to move it from its publicly accessible location to Jeff's private closet. In the middle of the day, Saul, Dan, and I picked up the fridge and carried it out into the hall. For a moment we considered where to put it.

"My office?" Dan suggested hopefully, to the disapproval

of the rest of us. "Up in the false ceiling where Matthew used to stash dope?" That seemed more appropriate.

When the supply clerk came around, he smelled a rat. Summoning one of the security guards, he ran from office to office demanding, "Okay. Where did ya put it? Who's got it?"

"Got what?" we shrugged and went back to work. "Listen, Mac," I said, "can't you leave me alone? Can't you see I am trying to do something *creative*?"

After our escapade was over Saul commented to me, "Can you believe it? Status symbols among monks. This is some 'New Age.' These new-style renunciates aren't after the traditional holier-than-thou, I-threw-more-ashes-on-my-food-than-you type of leverage. They want *things,* and lots of them. They want what other executives have got—Pierre Cardin suits, big offices, and a sweet young lady typing up memos on an IBM Selectric. I hate men, they are all alike."

Shortly after Jeff arrived, our most itinerant comrade also came to town. This was Charles Cameron, the DLM writer who edited *Who Is Guru Maharaj Ji?,* a paperback put out by Bantam in 1973. Though Charles thought of himself as a poet first, I got the impression that he didn't really like to write at all. What he really loved was touring the country and speaking on college campuses about art and spirituality. He loved to read his poems to big audiences, tell stories, do impersonations. He was very good at this, too. Telling a sad story, he could make me cry. Charles was British. He had gone to Oxford and his poems had been published in the volume *The Children of Albion.* Another quality I distinctly remember about Charles was his insatiable admiration of women. Though when it came down to "Shall I or shan't I" have sex, he confessed that he almost always backed down and kept his monastic vows. But to hear him talk publicly you'd get quite the opposite impression.

When Charles arrived in town, he was discouraged with our new situation. He shook his head and said, "First fanatics and then bureaucrats. Our mission gets harder every year."

However, Charles had a plan. He came to one of the writers' meetings and said with his British accent, "An artist is like no other individual. He or she [at the word "she" Charles gazed around the room at the young women present] must use this difference for the advantage of the world. We need *divine subversion* in this organization. You can see the trends. You know what *they* [he cast his eyes dramatically skyward toward the direction of the executive offices] want us to do. Boring things, without life, without art, without love." On the word love, Charles's eyes traveled around the room again to the females present at the meeting. "Only we, the artists of DLM, can revive their lifeless ways."

None of us shared Charles's utter and incontrovertible high opinion of our own vocations. We did not fancy ourselves to be a group of latter-day Prometheuses. But a little divine subversion was just our speed. After this day the R&D department quietly became a cosmic version of "Spanky and Our Gang."

According to Michael's organizational charts we were to research and develop ideas which would inform and inspire the premies through the magazine and newspaper, and attract the general public to DLM through films, brochures, and leaflets. The arrow leading away from the R&D box on Michael's charts indicated the flow of our energy was to leave headquarters. Instead, we planned to reverse the flow: Send our energy up the ladder, and do a little CR * work upstairs.

As Gandhi pointed out, nonviolent tactics only work in a country where the people in charge have certain, however slight, humanistic sympathies. That is why Martin Luther King's peaceful civil disobedience worked here in the United States. In the same way, yippie theater only works when played to an audience that is ready to laugh. That's why

---

* That's Consciousness-Raising, for those of you who slept through the sixties.

I was a serious threat to the principal of Friends Academy. The schoolkids who were my contemporaries were always ready to laugh at a good gag. In DLM, yippie strategy took on a new dimension. The thing to remember about our R&D chief, Jeff Grossberg, was that he wasn't really an ogre. He had joined DLM because he did not want to be an executive. Meditation had given him a satisfaction status had not.

Jeff was not an organization man at heart, and neither were the other "professional" managers. But somewhere along the line, between 1971 and now, 1975, they had lost their original motivation in joining DLM, traded it in for a fancy suit. If DLM was to realize its goals, then our leaders would have to go through some changes.

In March 1975, Bob Mishler—still DLM president through all the organizational shifts—came back from a long tour he had been on with Maharaj Ji. During the whole reorganization he had been out of the country. While he was away, he had done some thinking. It was time for another publicity campaign, he decided. The public and the press were ready for DLM and Maharaj Ji to come out of the closet again. He wanted something ecumenical, something light. No heavy-duty dogma, no "Lord has come" crap. Just our message: Knowledge can help you gain profound insight into life.

"The way you can come up with a campaign," Bob told us in a meeting to which none of the other "executives" were invited, "is to get into a creative space. Meditate and dream. Do it together. I may not seem like much of an artist, but I know that a group of creative people can experience powerful communication together. I want you to get into it completely. Do not tell anybody your group's thinking. Keep it a secret until it is done. Otherwise your energy and enthusiasm will leak away. Don't tell your roommates. Don't tell me. Don't tell the other directors. This is your show. Do something that you, yourself, would like to give out, as a gift, on the streets."

Giving us only these general instructions, Bob left town to travel with Maharaj Ji to a mini-festival in Florida, and then after Florida, to India, where Maharaj Ji was going to confront the Mata Mafia. What I did not know at this time was that a gap was growing between Bob and the other directors. They resented his single-handed style and his closeness to Maharaj Ji. If they had been giving us directions rather than Bob, we would have probably gotten quite different guidelines for the new campaign.

Here was our chance, we thought, to say what we really felt our organization should be like. Now, with Bob behind us, we could do it, come up with a well-reasoned solution to the bureaucratic spirit we found engulfing the Mission. Right away we went to work in hermit-like seclusion. Bob had told us that there was no deadline on our work; we had as long as we needed to do it right. But once Bob was out of town, the remaining members of the executive group started to put pressure on us to come up with a campaign right away. Curtailing our leisure, we started contemplating double-time. By April we had the basic theme for a national campaign.

The main idea of it was based on C. S. Lewis's concept that you could lead people into higher awareness ("God," in his words) through art and beauty, which he said were imitations of the supreme. We wanted everything DLM did —from mailings to local directors, to the public campaigns— to be light, beautiful art objects. We wanted them to be full of fun and not to take themselves too seriously. For each area of mission activities we had specific suggestions, but no finished mock-ups. After much debate, the brainstorming team decided that our head designer, an attractive woman named Joan Boykin, should present it to the almost exclusively male executive group. "After all," as our British poet, Charles, said, "Joanie is the one among us who looks most like a piece of art."

Joan took the idea upstairs, expecting an enthusiastic reception. "But after I explained it to them," she said, "they were all quiet. They just looked at me. After a minute Michael Dettmers said, 'Thank you, Joan, you can go.' "

That was the last time we heard about our campaign for almost six weeks. In the meantime, Guru Maharaj Ji was back in the headlines in newspapers around the world. While Maharaj Ji was in India, Mata had denounced him as a "playboy." She declared that it was really BB who was the Satguru, Lord of All. Now sure that God was on her side, she also started out trying to gain legal control of DLM and sole rights to the actual name, "Divine Light Mission." Let her have it, I thought.

Not knowing the fate of our campaign-reform effort, but suspecting the worst, most of the R&D staff went back to work on their ongoing concerns while waiting for the executive group's decision. Dan had a burst of enthusiasm about our next newspaper. A populist by nature, Dan had been inspired by then *Harper's Magazine*'s contributing editor Tony Jones' revival of *Harper's Weekly*. What Tony Jones wanted to do was publish a paper which was written by the readers. Dan felt the *Divine Times* needed similar refurbishment; it was too headquarters-oriented. Even with all of my efforts in national news, I agreed with him.

Too often the executives would tell Jeff they wanted a certain editorial or a certain interview (often with themselves) to go into the *Divine Times* so that the premies would become aware of the executives' latest organizational ideas. Dan and I were not so sure "mission trends," as we tactfully called the exec-ordered articles, were what the readers wanted. In plans for the coming issue Dan included a survey, as part of a large section encouraging reader participation, which he called "It's Your Paper!"

One of my assignments for this issue was an interview with an old friend of mine, Ellen Saxl, who had escorted Maharaj Ji on his trip to India. Incidentally, Ellen was one of the first people from an Eastern-oriented spiritual group to be kidnapped by "de-programmer" Ted Patrick, whose usual quarry was Christian cults. However, Ellen was not "de-programmed," and later her court testimony helped to convict Patrick of kidnapping. While my interview with Ellen seemed, at first glance, to be a simple assignment, it brought up some disturbing questions.

Ellen and I had lunch together and then sat down with the Sony to talk. She described the trip in glowing terms: The scenery, the people she met, the beautiful premies, Maharaj Ji's one triumph after another over the Mata mafia. However, as she spoke, her looks and gestures and tone told another story. She fidgeted, seemed uncomfortable.

"Is there something wrong?" I asked her. "Don't you feel well?"

"Turn off the tape recorder," she said urgently, as if I was about to be let in on some of the state secrets. I obliged. "Sophia, the trip was awful. Premies were beaten. Maharaj Ji was in hiding for a week in this crummy hotel. And the lawsuit which Mata brought, I don't know if we won. Raja Ji may have to go to jail if he ever goes back . . ." Ellen continued unfolding a tale of horror.

"But why are you telling me this other story? Why were you giving me this baloney?"

"Because that's what Maharaj Ji wanted. I asked him, 'When I return, Maharaj Ji, what shall I tell people?' And he said, 'Just talk about the grace.' Sophia, there *were* good things that happened. The huge second wedding celebration Maharaj Ji held. About five thousand premies were there . . . good things and bad both."

"But why not give the whole story? Premies can handle it. It's no big deal."

"I'm honor-bound," Ellen said. "I promised Maharaj Ji.

Sometimes we don't always know the reasons for things he tells us to do, but from my experience, if I just do them, I get good results."

"All right then, I'll turn the tape recorder back on and you tell the story however you like. I can't compel you otherwise."

And so Ellen continued weaving a bright tale, rich with cultural references and local color. She remembered so many beautiful things—the filigree on a certain building, the oxcarts and peasants in a certain town—but this story did not move me, now that I knew the other side.

When Ellen left, I sat alone. I wondered why Maharaj Ji did not want the truth known. Already AP, the wire service, had carried parts of what he wished to suppress. Unlike Ellen, I *did* feel the need to understand the reasoning behind an action before I took it. I could not see any good reason for Maharaj Ji's request "only to talk about the grace."

During the week, while Ellen's "interview" was being transcribed, we got the news about our campaign. Thumbs down. During their six weeks of silence the executive group had been creating their own campaign. But since they could not come up with a suitable slogan, they agreed to use a modified version of the worst of our many suggestions, on one or two posters. The slogan used was, "Discover the Sunny Kingdom of Heaven Inside Through Meditation." Trying to create a feeling of solidarity, we sent one of the executives a memo telling him we were behind him on the new campaign, but in my heart as I signed the note, I felt disappointed.

To make it worse for Dan and me, the "It's Your Paper" idea was also panned, along with the new campaign. Dan received a rather curt memo that said, basically, he had no business giving the paper to the premies. It was "Maharaj Ji's paper for his message." The executive group didn't want to print "any old thing" premies sent in. They wanted to "guide" the development of the communities nationwide.

A few days later, I caught a ride home with Dettmers and another executive.

"What was the matter with the R&D campaign?" I asked them. Like Joanie, I was greeted with silence.

Finally Michael Dettmers spoke. "It isn't quite what we had in mind."

The other executive continued, expressing the group's sentiment. "We needed something a little more mature, less fantasy."

"Right," Dettmers finished. "A little more like a bank."

"A bank?" My eyes filled with tears. Here were the "creative leaders" I put my faith in. Wanting to appeal to a higher authority, I wondered why Maharaj Ji didn't take a more active interest in the day-to-day affairs of DLM. Or maybe this is the way he wants things, I thought, feeling worse all the while. Seeing how upset I was, they tried to comfort me.

"Listen, we talked about hiring a PR firm to do the campaign but then we gave it to you guys. We're using your slogan. . . . It was just that the other parts were a little out of hand. You understand, don't you?"

I looked out the window. We were passing Humboldt Street, a few blocks down from the premie laundry. "Sure, I understand. Can you let me out here? I have to pick up my dry cleaning." I got out of the car. Walking across the park on my way home, I met Saul. "Why are you walking? Where's the bike?" I asked him, referring to the ten-speed we shared.

"Someone stole the seat, can't use it like that," he answered as I took his arm and we walked together.

Even if the executives did not think "It's Your Paper" was the right motto for a DLM publication, the readers loved it. They started writing in immediately, sending stories, poems, articles, newspaper clippings, jokes, cartoons, you name it. Buoyed with this response, Dan could not be daunted by any killjoy executives.

"We'll do a *Divine Times* aimed at the public which will incorporate the ideas we came up with in March," he announced to me one morning as I came into his office. I cheered up when I saw Dan in this good mood. The two of us ran off to get some kefir, a bottled yogurt drink, and wander around Scribner's bookstore, our favorite place to think up new ideas. I was always amazed how Dan kept his spirits up. Everyone else in the R&D department, including me, seemed to be rather deflated after the campaign was shot down.

While our "public" *Divine Times* project was still in the idea stage, Jeff recruited someone to act as his assistant and to be in charge of our writing staff. The person he found was Sharon Stokke, a young organization woman, similar in style to himself. As the writing progressed, Sharon wanted to see every bit of it for "approval." After Sharon had arrived, the number of things that needed approval had multiplied tenfold. Eventually it got so that we couldn't even send a memo to another department without it passing over her desk and getting her initials. Certain communications needed both Jeff's and her initials. I honestly believe that Sharon liked me and felt I had some creative abilities, but when it came to approval she was a changed woman. Blue pencil in hand, she went over everything line by line while I sat by and watched. Her comments, like Jeff's, were most often not in the area of art, taste, or style. A Harold Ross she was not. Instead, her criticism was largely of my ideas.

I was too irreverent with Maharaj Ji, she said. "He's not an ordinary man with ordinary motivations such as you describe. He's special, superhuman in a way. You have to portray that." I was too casual about Knowledge. "Our path is actually the only one that will lead people to truth, you know. We don't want to mislead anyone by making them think differently," Sharon told me in one of these "approval" sessions.

The whole business struck me as psychic brutality. I defended what I had written on the basis of my experience. Sharon was ready to put aside everything I felt if it did not fit into her version of the Divine Light Mission theology. Sometimes leaving Sharon's office I felt so confused I broke down and cried. I stopped in to Dan's office to be comforted. Resting my head against his big chest, I wondered why things were going like this.

"Do you think this is what Maharaj Ji wants?" I asked Dan one day in frustration after some of his and my collaborative articles were "edited" by Jeff Grossberg in not only a gross but also apparently propagandistic way.

"I don't know, Sophia. My general feeling is that Maharaj Ji doesn't pay much attention to what's going on here in Denver. His 'hands off' policy about our day-to-day work says to me, 'Okay, kids, you have the Knowledge. You know how to tune into the wisdom inside yourself, now try and do it!' "

"I hope that's right, Dan, but after what happened with Ellen I've been wondering if 'hands off' is just a way of avoiding the problems he doesn't want to deal with. Maybe Maharaj Ji is behind these people—Sharon, Jeff, and the others—but he doesn't come out and say it. He lets them do the dirty work."

"Hmmm." Dan looked down at his desk. I could see the thought had crossed his mind also.

In September 1975, it was a year since I had decided to come back to DLM and give it a second try. In spite of the intense conflicts, I was glad I had rejoined the mission. I had formed six or seven friendships which were deeper than any I had known before. Professionally, I had been exposed to a wider range of experiences than a nineteen-year-old working in any other company might have. From my work on the newspaper I had learned what it takes to get an idea out of your head and onto the printed page. I knew how a graphics studio should be set up. In a pinch I could operate a typesetting machine or a copy camera. A printing press was no mystery to me. I felt at home casually chatting in printing jargon, conversing about color overlays versus color separations, explaining the difference between signatures and flats, or determining what percentage a screen was.

From my work on DLM films I had learned the basics about that medium also. I understood how a recording studio was set up. I could scramble after a microphone and plug it into a sixteen-track mixing console with the best of them. I had seen film edited and knew how a KEM table, the Rolls-Royce of editing boards, worked.

If nothing else, in DLM I'd gotten a good education and made some good friends. To top this off, it had cost very little beyond the value of my labor and time. None of these personal and professional benefits was why I joined DLM, but they seemed like a good enough reason to stick around. Looking on the bright side, I could hope, like any employee who wants to keep a job, that things would improve; that the corporate closed-mindedness would pass, as the Millennium Fever had. It did not occur to me until later that what afflicted Sharon/Jeff/Michael Dettmers et al might be the Millennium Fever in a new form.

Toward the end of the autumn our main project was the publication of materials for a large festival we were planning for Orlando, Florida. We worked very hard and enjoyed a good relationship with Sharon. Schedules were so tight, we didn't have time for the same "approvals" process we had during the production of the public *Divine Times*. Most of our lighthearted copy was okayed without a question.

The festival was completely different from Millennium; BB wasn't there. It was held in a big field in Orlando, and about twelve thousand people attended. There was no hype. It was not billed as anything other than a nice time to get together, see Maharaj Ji, see your friends, take a vacation in Florida. Saul and I went to Disneyworld and spent a day, playing on the rides. It was lovely to be in the sun, relax, swim, and see old friends. Maharaj Ji gave beautiful addresses on three successive evenings. The third night I felt so moved, I cried. I forgave him for his lack of ability to manage DLM more effectively. He was trying, I could see that.

On the last day in November, I got a package in the mail from my friend who sends me *The New York Times*. Among other clippings was something that caught my attention. It was from William James:

> When a religion has become an orthodoxy, its day of inwardness is over; the spring is dry, the faithful live at second hand exclusively and stone the prophets in their turn. The new church, in spite of whatever human goodness it may foster, can be henceforth counted on as a staunch ally in every attempt to stifle the spontaneous religious spirit, and to stop all later bubblings of the fountain from which in purer days it drew its own supply of inspiration. . . .
>
> The plain fact is that men's minds have many other things in them besides their religion, and unholy entanglements and associations inevitably obtain. The basenesses so commonly charged to religion's account are thus, almost all of them, not chargeable at all to religion proper, but rather to religion's wicked practical partner, the spirit of corporate dominion. And the bigotries are most of them in their turn chargeable to religion's wicked intellectual partner, the spirit of dogmatic dominion, the passion for laying down the law in the form of an absolutely closed-in theoretic system. The ecclesiastical spirit in general is the sum of these two spirits of dominion; and I beseech you never to confound the phenomena of mere tribal or corporate psychology which it presents with those manifestations of the purely interior life. . . .

Thinking about our situation from this angle, I went down to one of the nightly programs DLM held. At these programs almost anybody could arrange to speak for a few minutes if they made an appointment weeks in advance. Usually I did not attend. Instead, I liked to spend my nights at home reading or talking with Barbara-Casey, my roommate and co-worker in R&D. When I arrived at the program I listened intently, trying to hear if there was an ecclesiastical spirit working on the general membership. I wanted to know if they suffered in subtle ways under a system of "approvals" such as I had found working under Sharon.

The first speaker was a young woman. She described her day at work and "all the little ways Guru Maharaj Ji had been teaching her things" while she washed dishes at a restaurant for two dollars an hour. She said she had received Knowledge four months before and had never seen Guru Maharaj Ji in person, but after attending *satsang* she had been able to "feel his presence. . . . There have been so many coincidences I just know Guru Maharaj Ji is with me all the time."

The next speaker was an older woman, a premie and the mother of two DLM members. She told about a dream she had where she met one of the mahatmas on a path and he looked at her and smiled. "You know, I've had Knowledge a long time, but I didn't experience what the other premies seemed to feel in meditation. This dream reassures me I'm on the path too."

Another person, a young man: "I hope one day my mom will take Knowledge, too. I've spoken to both my folks about it, and I don't know how they can resist truth. Knowledge is working so powerfully in the world, I don't know how anybody can miss it."

After three or four more testimonies the program was over. One of the later speakers echoed something that sounded Sharon-esque. "I've been going down to the Ananda Marga spiritual group and they say that sometimes a master guru comes to earth with a great spiritual mission. I feel like I'm infiltrating that group so I can tell them the good news. The Master is here and his name is Guru Maharaj Ji."

Walking home alone, I thought over these things. Somehow it reminded me of Pop art. A few years before, when I was at The Museum of Modern Art in Manhattan, I sat on a bench and watched people drift past one of Andy Warhol's compositions. Each group had its own interpretation. Each found some way to see a pattern, some order or meaning in this ordinary-appearing canvas. The reason they bothered to do this, I felt, was because of the weight and authority of The Museum of Modern Art. Equally fine patterns could be seen in the supermarket.

Somehow, in the same way that the curators of MOMA had induced the public to find order in the work of Andy Warhol, DLM was giving authority to Guru Maharaj Ji. The first premie who spoke had seen how Maharaj Ji was moving the forces in her life. I felt this was true only in the most symbolic sense—all Maharaj Ji was doing, as far as I could see, was sitting back in Malibu and getting fat. When the older woman could not see the order her children found, she assumed the deficiency was in her, just as the yokels who wander into The Museum of Modern Art assume they don't understand art.

The next two speakers were so confident in their perception of Knowledge and Maharaj Ji, they didn't feel the need to examine other people's lives and views for any true value. The young man who complained that his parents were resisting truth was the son of two Ph.D.'s, one in Greek classics and the other in political science. Perhaps they were equally smug in their correctness as their son was in his, but I would imagine they'd still have some insight to share. Ananda Marga is a group much like DLM, except it lacks a corporate style. From them, too, I imagine we could learn a lot, if we listened for their wisdom, rather than for the right moment to hit them with the truth: "The Master is here . . ."

"Damn," I thought. "Every group on the street thinks they've got the truth. The Krishna people say, 'I don't think Krishna is Lord, I *know*.' The Children of God say the same thing. Everybody *knows*. Everybody *knows*. There must be a hundred thousand gods that people are worshipping, and a lot of good it has done us, ever, in this world."

When I got home I went right to bed. Sleeping, I had bad dreams.

CHAPTER
17

IT WAS JANUARY 1976, THE MIDDLE OF THE WINTER, BUT STILL I had that spring feeling. A few days before I had returned to Denver from visiting friends back East. I had taken a train trip through New England, where I had become thoroughly steeped in winter's presence. Everywhere had been cold: Ice had covered all of the Connecticut streams; through New Hampshire there were frozen fields blanketed with snow; in Maine the trees were black, wet, and bare.

Yet even today, as snow was falling in large flakes from the sky, dark at midday, it felt like spring. I wanted to leap up, dance on my desk top, kick out the jams, find some sweet person, and fall in love.

Where, in this unlikely season, did I get this feeling? Maybe it blew in from Mexico across the Rocky Mountains. Or maybe I caught a whiff of it as I opened up a crate of green buttercrunch lettuce while I was helping down at the co-op. I was wondering about all of these things when Dan came into my little office—Saul and I had both moved to separate but adjoining rooms, so mostly these days I was alone with the window. From the look in Dan's eye, I could see he had that spring feeling too.

"Hey, bear," I said to him, noticing that in a way he looked like the gentle sort of bear cub Smokey must have been before Smokey traded in his wildlife independence for shovel, trousers, and national recognition on buses and billboards across America.

Dan sat down in my visitor's chair and I noticed the spiffy way he was dressed: nice suit with a shirt open at the neck, but no fancy shoes. His outfit was bottomed off by his old Adidas running shoes, just the same as I wore. At nineteen years, I was still in sneakers.

After a minute I could see that the business bringing Dan to my office was not commas and colons, the editor's usual concern, but instead, Cadbury bars, fancy chocolate that comes wrapped in foil for twenty cents.

"Got some time?" Dan asked me.

"Sure, but the snow . . ."

"We'll run." He was confident, as young men often are who've been over six feet since before they were fourteen.

Dan was first and I was next as we zipped down to the street in a lightning flash, two blocks to the Hilton, in whose cafe we often sat to eat our chocolate bars, square by square. Chocolate has xanthines in it, the same drug that adds the zip to coffee, tea, and Coca-Cola. Eating chocolate Dan and I get stoned, our senses perhaps refined through our ashram abstinence from the harder stuff.

What William James had seen in 1905 and what my friend could see from across the country, Dan and I could see from where we sat. DLM was already showing the signs. It had become an "ecclesiastical institution" beset with all the maladies James described.

But for me and Dan it was different than for James or my friend who sends me *The New York Times*. We were in the middle of it. We had devoted three years to building something which was turning out to be nothing more than another religion. We had made a noble effort to turn the tide with yippie tricks and reasoned talk and even tears, but still, we could see what had happened. The organization had tens of thousands of solid members, people who had joined in good faith, attracted by the promise that meditation would tune them into their inner nature, but who had become rank and file in a new religion. How did this happen? Dan and I needed to know.

"Look." Dan pulled out of his pocket some notes he'd made from reading Thomas Kuhn's *Structure of Scientific Revolutions.* "We have to try to understand the nature of the mind. People's minds make theories to explain what they see. But these theories are just models, incomplete renditions of reality. Gradually, though, people forget that they are just theories. They write texts as though the theories are truth. People get cushy. They think they've got the story locked up tight. Then they try to suppress new facts that aren't explained by the theory. And when they can't suppress them any longer, then they *puzzle* solve, they invent ways, logical constructions which could explain how the theory is still true even in the light of contradictory evidence. What they don't do is *problem* solve, create a whole new paradigm to encompass all the new learning."

"But it seems to me, Dan, that despite all this, premies are always able to have access to the original material, through meditation, the wordless reality. You'd think a cosmology *wouldn't* be formed. You'd think the continual direct experience in meditation would correct false religious ideas . . ."

"Right, right!" Dan was getting more excited every minute. (Watch out for Cadbury bars.) "But you see, premies aren't meditating. I mean, they may make some effort, may sit down and watch their breath, but really, I feel they are only doing it to get a bit of peace—to relax, like it's some organic Valium. They falsely believe that they understand the truth. They are satisfied that they've already got the whole pie. I think the organization offers an artificial security which keeps people from doing their own realizing. From diving into the profound regions."

I thought about this and felt it was true. At the nightly programs DLM held in Denver, I heard people get up day after day and say the same things. People felt they had realized something when, finally, after much struggle, they had been able to accept the consensus; when finally, they believed. They accepted Maharaj Ji as a superior being, they saw themselves redeemed in his grace. . . .

"So what do you want me to do, get a Railpass and travel all over America telling people to meditate harder?"

"No, no, no. People will still puzzle solve, even though meditation gives them the facts. What I am saying means one thing. We've got to blow up DLM."

I agreed. We shook hands and then sat for a time, looking at the snow.

Ours was not as revolutionary a pronouncement as it may sound. After the festival many people were beginning to talk along the same lines. In the letters I received from my national news correspondents I sensed a mood of dissatisfaction in the DLM membership. Not only were they dissatisfied with the way the Mission was being run, but also with the quality of their own spiritual experience. I remember one particular letter from the retired financial director whom Michael Dettmers replaced. He was working in the Portland, Oregon, DLM office as a part-time volunteer. (Unfortunately I have had to reconstruct this letter from memory, as I lost the original; it is impossible to duplicate his charming style.)

We started by asking each other, "Why did you join DLM?" From this beginning we have traced through our whole DLM experience. Immediately it is evident that many of us have deeply entrenched religious concepts, almost totally without basis in experience. The people working in the local DLM office translate these baseless concepts into programs that encourage guilt and fear as the primary motivators, rather than love and clarity. Sometimes I wonder if it might just be better to cancel DLM and start again. I've heard several people say this here in Portland.

It had all started the month before, when Maharaj Ji

came to the Denver community meeting and said that all the people in DLM should have "understanding." He seemed very emphatic about this, although it was rather vague just exactly what he wanted people to understand. Each person, according to her/his nature, interpreted Maharaj Ji's statement differently. Michael Dettmers and some of the other executives assumed people on the HQ staff needed to understand the organization and their commitment to it more fully. To this end, in the middle of December, they set up a large conference for the entire staff at the Hilton Hotel. They secured the services of a premie who was a professional in group dynamics. Maharaj Ji came to the conference and told everybody that he was completely behind this effort and the premies should relax, cooperate, and "not be paranoid."

Predictably, half of the conference was taken up with addresses by the executive staff. A new organizational chart was revealed and explained at length. But the other half of the conference, put together on the suggestions of the group dynamics professional, was completely different. People split up into "task teams" to come up with answers to specific problems. The teams were then to write their solution on a large piece of paper and post it on the wall. Before beginning we were given a little talk about teamwork. Whatever solution we came to had to be a group conclusion; nobody was to be left out.

To make sure this happened, the idea was to work on both the "task," the specific problem in front of us, and the "maintenance," or feelings of involvement and openness in the group.

The first task was to complete this sentence: "Commitment to Divine Light Mission equals . . ." In the course of this it was impossible not to get into why each person had joined the Mission and what their experiences and frustrations had been; it even provided the opportunity to broach the very delicate issue of whether Guru Maharaj Ji had powers and abilities far beyond those of mortal men. Was Guru Maharaj Ji wiser than the rest of us, or was he just a sweet young man who was little more than a figurehead, a symbolic focus?

The reason this was such a delicate subject, I realized, was that many of the premies put up with the endless difficulties of DLM only because they believed Maharaj Ji had a plan; even if they could not see it, Maharaj Ji knew there was some meaning, reason, or ultimate justification for the scandal, difficulties, and grief they had seen over the several years of their involvement. Their reason for staying in DLM was based on him. They loved him, but they hardly knew him. If he was a fool, they were fools for staying with him for so long.

I and most of my close associates, on the other hand, did not feel our fates were so eternally bound with Maharaj Ji's. We had been attracted to the Mission for reasons other than him, and had decided to stay even after we saw his deficiencies.

When my group got around to this touchy issue, I found nobody wanted to be the little child who announced the emperor's nakedness. Even I didn't want to open the can of worms. Slowly, in the course of the team's functioning, I realized there was something I was not facing. Okay, I knew Maharaj Ji was not the hottest thing going, but I enjoyed being in the mission, personally and professionally. I still had hopes that things would get straightened out. But somewhere inside me, I knew that if I started getting deeply into questions about Maharaj Ji, I would reach a point where I would need to know with certainty what he thought about himself. Had he acquiesced mentally to all the adoration and begun to believe he was the Lord?

I knew that if I asked this question seriously I might just find out that Maharaj Ji did think he was God. And if that was indeed what he believed I would have to leave the Mission, leave my friends, leave my hopes, and start out anew.

There is no way I could stay around a mission led by a crazy man, no matter how clever, charming, and charismatic that man was.

Yet over the past year I had begun to suspect the worst. Inside I was straining to resolve my doubts. Today, in the Hilton, I knew I would begin. "I don't think he's God," I announced. "I don't think he's even got any special insight."

"But what are we doing here then?" someone else in my group asked me.

It was an obvious question. A debate ensued:

FIRST PERSON: There is something so marvelous I experience in meditation. Where did that come from? And when I see Maharaj Ji I feel a powerful energy. Remember that reporter from the *Denver Post*? Where did the golden light come from? Come on, you have to admit the kid's got some power.

ME: I don't know the answer. There are many things I don't know. The list grows longer every day.

THIRD PERSON: But I feel that too. I have doubts about Maharaj Ji. We give him a lot of money and don't seem to get much back.

FOURTH PERSON: How can you doubt? Maharaj Ji loves you so much. You people are so ungrateful for what he has done for you. He has taken us from unreality and shown us truth. Like Christ, he has delivered us. You know I was a junkie, before the Mission. The only thing that got me through was praying to Maharaj Ji. Now I'm off junk. Don't tell me he's not special.

We talked heatedly for several hours, the allotted time for the task, and came up with the sentence, "Commitment to DLM is commitment to Guru Maharaj Ji." It seemed true, but I felt both commitments slipping fast.

Elsewhere around the room, groups had found the same live wire. By the time the conference was over, many doubting Thomases had come out. Those who still harbored their doubts deep inside, a secret for only themselves to know, began thinking.

It was not what Michael Dettmers had planned, but in the following weeks everyone was still talking about the issues which had come up in the conference. "Listen, man, we've got to get down to basics. I feel you are hedging. Maharaj Ji's either God or he's not . . . " I heard the mail clerk tell the office messenger in the mail room.

By January, on the snowy day when Dan and I sat eating chocolate square by square in the Hilton, burning down DLM did not seem particularly revolutionary. It was something already happening in Denver; now it only needed to spread far and wide.

This was the one big clearance sale—everything must go. Naturally, as during any insurrection, there was a conservative faction, and a reactionary faction, too. They like it just fine the way it is, thank you. And they don't see any reason why we have to ruin it with all of our questions.

My personal question was, does Maharaj Ji actually think he's a divine figure? This seemed like the crux of the whole matter. Back in November I had written a little blurb for a brochure advertising the festival commemorating Hans' birthday. I had said, "This is a special occasion because it gives us a chance to see that Maharaj Ji is not only a Guru but also a premie, a person just like us." Somehow this slipped by Sharon and got printed in the *Divine Times*. Once it had been run off ten thousand copies' worth, Jeff came into my office and said, shaking his head, "You really blew it this time. You really did."

"Why, what's the trouble?"

"Maharaj Ji's no premie, stupid. When Bob saw the newspaper, he called the Boss. There's no way he's going to release that issue of the paper saying he's a premie. We have to reprint and recollate."

Shaking his head, Jeff walked out. On one hand I felt

228

sorry I'd insulted Maharaj Ji, but, wow, did that sound like ego. Thinking about it now, toward the end of January, it seemed to be rather indicative. If Maharaj Ji wouldn't step off the stage for a minute, then maybe he was afraid—if the premies got one close look, it might ruin the magic.

But then, on the other hand, I remembered a story I heard from Freddy, the absentminded porter who forgot BB's suitcase full of money on the airport runway.

Maharaj Ji liked to watch movies. Sometime in 1973 Freddy had shown Maharaj Ji a Hollywood comedy called *The Mouse That Roared,* starring Peter Sellers in the role of a bumbling prince of a tiny country. In this tiny country the main occupation was wine making. Because a California vineyard had recently come out with a cheap imitation of its main product, the country was facing a dreadful recession. Hours of cabinet meetings with the Queen Mother suggested no solution. Then the prince had an inspiration. "We must declare war on the United States," he announced. According to his scheme, their country would declare war and forthwith lose. Then, undoubtedly, American aid would pour in and the country would experience the same prosperity as other countries that had lost wars to the United States, such as Japan or Germany.

The countrypeople were delighted and prepared for war, bringing out crossbows and chain-mail armors. They sailed to New York and went ashore, only to find the entire city deserted. Unknown to the prince and his soldiers, an air raid drill was in progress. As it happened, the only people around were an absentminded professor and his beautiful daughter. They were working on the professor's invention—a very powerful weapon called the Q-Bomb.

Seeing his opportunity, the prince captured the beautiful daughter and her father. Then he called his mother and told her that he had won the war. Meanwhile the beautiful daughter and the prince fell in love.

When they got back to their border they found an envoy from every powerful nation waiting for them, begging for the bomb. After many negotiations, the bomb started ticking menacingly. The professor took it back to the makeshift lab he had set up and attempted to disarm it. At a crucial moment a tiny mouse crawled out. The professor looked quizzically at the bomb and asked, in a classic Hollywood German accent, "Are you a dud?" The prince, the beautiful daughter, and the professor made a pact of silence. Because people continued to believe the three of them had the Q-Bomb they were able to direct the world onto a more noble course.

When Maharaj Ji saw this film, he was thrilled. "This is exactly what I am doing," he said. "I've got the Knowledge Bomb."

This story indicated to me that Maharaj Ji did not think he was God; he understood that he was a bumbling prince whose claim to power was a placebo called Knowledge. In order to get Knowledge to work he had to talk it up, act as though it were a cosmic mystery, "the holiest of all secrets."

This approach had some merits. Peak experiences of the sort I had in early spring of 1973 are completely different from ordinary consciousness. When someone has one of these experiences he usually believes it is beyond his ability to have it again. He attributes his temporary high awareness to luck, fate, the stars, or perhaps he is just baffled by it.

A guru knows that most people have great unused potential. Essentially, the guru tricks the people who come to him into doing what they are already able to do. Just like the good doctor with the sugar pill. "Take this and you'll feel better soon."

If you are tempted to laugh at people who are cured by placebos, hold on. If you have ever taken cold pills and gotten relief, the joke's on you, too. According to an FDA study, when the government took a look at those tiny time pills they found "little evidence of any effect on major cold symptoms, except for minor decongestant action: It is ineffective as a fixed combination."

When the drug companies were confronted with this and similar studies, they "failed to substantiate claims for effectiveness [to] prevent or relieve the symptoms of a cold," according to the FDA's report. Still, they stand by their product. Speaking for the average consumer, the president of the drug industry lobby said, "If you find a product that works for you, then you *know* it works." The overwhelming public response to cold pills spoke louder to him than any study.

Spiritual experience is not like a cold cure. Once you've realized something, your growth is forever, unlike a cold, to which you'll be victim again and again. Because his students grow and learn, there comes a time when the guru trickster must let them graduate, must tell them the secret: "It was you all along. I tricked you into making the effort you needed to get you this far, but you did it *yourself*, you walked every step of the way."

Another fact in Maharaj Ji's favor was that he seemed to be encouraging a spring revolution, graduation in June. Or perhaps he was sick of being a big-time guru and wanted to settle down and be just folks.

"Once again life is following art," my father said when I told him of the situation, reminding me of a book by D. H. Lawrence. This novel suggests that Christ did not die on the cross, but rather fainted. Later, when he awakened in the tomb, he escaped and began a new life, feeling his mission was complete.

All of this controversy made me tremendously happy. Dan did a whole issue of the newspaper about "understanding," encouraging everyone to throw out their assumptions, question all their premises, and get back rooted in their real experiences. By the middle of February, Jeff wanted to get in on this new open awareness which was surging through his department.

As if to purge himself, he fired Sharon and became the newest member of R&D's cosmic Spanky and Our Gang. He put Saul in charge of us, as he was by every estimation the senior member of the writing staff. Immediately Saul abolished the post of "editor" and said everything should be done in a team approach. We formed the Divine Times Task Team and started cooking up articles to further the Spring Revolution among *DT* readers. "I Was a Happy Darkie for Guru Maharaj Ji," "Confessions of a Fanatic," and "Why I Left the Ashram," were just a few of the titles with which we hoped to arouse people's thoughts.

In forming the Divine Times Team we recruited someone from "North American Operations," the national coordinating department which communicated over the WATS lines with the local affiliates. We hoped this person could act as a news gatherer and save the postage and effort I had been expending to get the national news. Now that the "cultural revolution" had come to DLM, we wanted to make sure we got last-minute dispatches from The Front, the premie communities where the real changes would have to happen. Since North American Operations had the power of the WATS line and a full vice president as their director, they considered *Divine Times* small change. They assigned us one of the low-authority staff people. However, as soon as they saw the explosive list of articles we wanted to print, they became worried and sent some of their heavier brass in to watch over us.

"The *Divine Times* is actually an NAO function," they said, "because it is communicating to the North American premie community. Therefore we, rather than anybody down at R&D, should have the approval power over the articles."

Saul was incensed. He went straight to Jeff and told him, "Look, if you *are* behind us, work this out. We can't go on like this. It is completely contrary to the new way we are doing things."

Dan also spoke to Jeff about NAO. Dan understood the conflict as a struggle between an authoritarian style of management and a participatory style. "An authoritarian style will naturally inhibit the growth of consciousness. The Chief lays down the law for the workers, and they better do it no matter what they think. The Mission has been dominated by this style since it began. Now, Jeff," Dan spoke powerfully, "you have reached a point where *you* realize this is contradictory to our goal of promoting the growth of awareness. You are the only one who can help us. You have to go to bat for us with NAO."

Two weeks later, I was meditating in my room before dinner when I heard Barbara-Casey crying under her meditation blanket. In the half-light I could see tissue after tissue piling up on the floor.

"Barbara," I whispered to her, "are you crying?"

No answer. "Barbara . . . Barbara . . ." I went over to her bed and lay down on it. The only other time I had seen her cry was during a crisis period in her family.

She pulled the blanket off her. "Sophia, promise not to tell anybody until Thursday. Jeff's been fired."

Tears streamed down my face, too. I could see the executives were never going to relinquish their power. There would never be any participatory management structure in the Mission. There'd be no June graduation. This must be the way Maharaj Ji wants it—after all, he keeps these people in power, I thought as I put on my gloves and scarf, ready to break my promise to Barbara and walk over to Saul's to tell him the news. Whatever leeway Maharaj Ji had gained with me in Orlando, he had lost now.

It was an awkward time to fire Jeff. He'd been planning a retreat for the R&D staff. "Since we're going to be working together on everything from now on," he had explained when he suggested the idea a few weeks earlier, "don't you think we ought to get to know each other a little better?" He'd taken some of the department money and rented a lodge, cross-country skis, the works. But with the news of his dismissal, a shadow was cast across our weekend in the hills.

When we arrived at the lodge, we were served an amazingly good meal by one of the artists. After dinner we sang songs and watched old movies. Outside was a bright moon. With the films over, several people went out to take walks. I was about to join them when Terry, one of the artists, asked to walk with me. I'd felt a great deal of affection for Terry ever since 1973, when we'd met in one enchanting moment across Saul's desk. For two and a half years I had kept this attraction to myself, trying to keep in mind that I was a nun. Because Terry showed a "saintly" character, often meditating long hours and giving inspired talks at staff meetings, he had already been selected as a candidate for mahatma. (Maharaj Ji had recently chosen four western mahatmas.) I was surprised and happy when I found I would have his company.

The snow was a beautiful blue, reflecting the moon and sky. The pine branches were weighted down and sagging under the snow's weight. Silently we walked through the woods. I was tongue-tied. After a time we sat down on an old hollow log. "I think we've been hiding ourselves from each other," he said.

I was not about to confess what *I'd* been hiding. I said quickly, "What have you been hiding?"

"That I want to kiss you. That I love you."

I had to consider what to do for a minute, but my loving nature got the best of me. I nestled my head against his chest and then turned my face toward his. When we kissed, it was so sweet to feel once again the soft warmth of another person touching me. "I've loved you too, for almost three years."

234

"I've wanted to tell you how I felt ever since that day—do you remember when we met on the fifth floor in November, after Millennium?" Terry answered.

We kissed again and walked back to the lodge holding hands. The next day was warm. We walked way up high on a ridge where the snow was gone. The ground was dry and we lay down to make love on the hill in the sun.

Once we got back to town, I was not sure whether we should continue our physical relationship. I felt as long as I was in the ashram I should try to keep my vows, but soon I abandoned this line of reasoning. The relationship with Terry had such a beautiful effect on me that I wanted to feel it deeply in every way I could. The feeling of lying in this lover's arms was so soothing, it made me forget all the disappointment I had suffered with the Mission. In an astoundingly short time, I felt like a *completely* new person.

In the next few weeks, I had no heart to fight North American Operations, quibbling over phrasing, when I went to work. I wasn't bitter or weary. Suddenly I felt it had nothing to do with me. Sitting in a meeting with Dan and the NAO director was like listening to a family fight among neighbors that came, muffled, through the walls of an apartment. I might listen, but more often I wouldn't. It didn't concern me. If Maharaj Ji wanted to run a little religion based on his father's teachings and he was able to find people to join, so what? That was his business, not mine. It all seemed so simple. When I walked around the office I felt peculiarly free. I had great affection for many of these people, but my destiny was no longer tied to theirs.

From this detached and happy perspective, it was easy for me to see the trouble wasn't so much in the way DLM was doing things, but in what DLM was doing in the first place. By teaching people meditation it was encouraging them to be individuals of spirit, but in trying to organize them to specific tasks, it was not giving them room to be individuals of action. It was like putting Bill Buckley out to work on the Yangtze River commune in China. There was just no way for it to work out.

So, with no regrets, I decided to leave the organization and strike out on my own beckoning frontier. On my twentieth birthday, the 13th of March, 1976, I wrote a little resignation message and posted it in the office lunchroom. I called my mother and told her I was going to leave. She said she'd send me money for my fare home and asked if I'd like to spend the summer in East Hampton with her.

"You could grow a garden," she said. "Georgica Beach lost several feet last winter, but I go down and look at it every day. The water's still cold, but in June we can swim."

Georgica Beach? I thought. It will be good to go back where this all began. It took me until the first week in April to get everything ready and pack up my clothes and office to ship home. Terry spent almost all the time with me. He was thinking he might leave, too, but he'd go west; home to him was California.

I knew I'd miss him and all the people I loved in DLM, but I was sure that, whatever friends I left here, I'd have an equal number and more in the future. "Besides, who wants all their friends to be from the same guru cult, anyway?" Saul quipped as he saw me off. I went to the train station to catch the six o'clock through Chicago to New York. I looked back once and saw the skyline against the pale but deepening blue of the evening sky.

The next morning I woke up earlier than anyone. The sun had not yet come up over the vast brown dirt fields of Nebraska. As the sun broke over the horizon, I felt overwhelmed with joy. I took a pad out of my purse and wrote a poem, the first one in two years:

> No birds, this morning's dawn
> just the train
> and miles of new plowed fields
> unseeded yet.

When I got to New York it was eleven, two mornings later. I was so delighted to see the Big Apple, I went to a commuters' bar to have a beer. Stepping up boldly, I put my foot on the brass rail and ordered. I was the only woman in the place; my gusto must have made my voice loud. Up and down the bar the men's heads turned. I raised my mug in the air and gave them my biggest smile. Many of them returned the toast, raising their steins and drinking deep.

CONCLUSION

ELEVEN MONTHS HAVE PASSED SINCE I LEFT DIVINE LIGHT Mission. As it turned out, I did spend the summer with my mother in East Hampton. Several chapters of this book were written sitting on the sand at Georgica Beach, using a square driftwood beam for a desk. Saul, Dan, Barbara-Casey, Charles, even old Jeff all left Divine Light Mission shortly after I did. Right before leaving, most of the R&D group were offered jobs as organizers in the Carter campaign. Only two accepted. "One savior's enough," Saul explained. Saul moved to Boulder and is thinking about going to the university there. Dan and Barbara-Casey moved to California, as did Terry, and the two of them live together in Oakland. As a favor to me, Barbara-Casey came to New York and stayed with me for six weeks to type this manuscript. Charles went back to England, and I ran into Jeff on the street in Greenwich Village. Over pizza, he told me he planned to get married and settle down in Atlanta.

Bob Mishler left the organization toward the end of 1976.

I visited him in Denver and we spent a week together talking about what had happened to our original vision for Divine Light Mission, and why. His insight and candor were invaluable to me in preparing this book. A few days ago I saw Bob in New York; he is trying to start a film company and has already found some potential backers. Rennie Davis is still one of the DLM faithful, although he no longer lives in the ashram. He is married and has a job selling life insurance. Guru Maharaj Ji, himself, is up to the same old game. Struggling to keep the movement together, he has been touring extensively within the United States.

As for me, I live with my best friend in a beautiful apartment in a lovely part of New York called Brooklyn. My place has hardwood parquet floors, all the original detail from the building's turn-of-the-century construction, and loads of sunlight. In the bay window of my living room, I have built huge window boxes and am growing vegetables. In another month I am going to harvest some of the most fantastic salad in New York.

Now that this book is finished, there are so many things I want to do. I've started reading Arnold Toynbee's *Study of History* in an abridged version, but I'm enjoying it so much I want to continue on and read the whole twelve-volume set. I am currently designing some sculptures that look like people and have electronic sensors in them that will react to variations in the sculpture's environment. My mind is full of film ideas. Not only have I got a backlog of ideas from my old Research and Development days, but there are new scripts boiling around inside my head, waiting for me to stop working on my own story and get to work on theirs.

One of my oldest interests, politics, has surfaced again. I am keeping up with current developments on the national and international scene and thinking what I would do if I were sitting in the Oval Office. Watch out, some day I might be.

In general, I am extremely happy, still experimenting with living the best life, and feel very much like Newton, who said, ". . . in all of my work, I feel that I have been just a child playing with a shell by the side of the great ocean of truth."

And at twenty, that's a great way to feel.